VERMONT
SEASONINGS

Steve Delaney

VERMONT SEASONINGS

*Reflections on the Rhythms
of a Vermont Year*

Steve Delaney, R.F.

Illustrated by Amelia B. Fountain

PLAIDSWEDE PUBLISHING

Concord, New Hampshire

ISBN 978-0-9790784-3-9
Library of Congress Control Number: 2007931889

Designed and composed at Hobblebush Books,
Brookline, New Hampshire (www.hobblebush.com)

Printed in the United States of America

Cover design and illustration by Amelia B. Fountain

Published by:

PLAIDSWEDE PUBLISHING
P.O. Box 269 · Concord, New Hampshire 03302-0269
www.plaidswede.com

Many of the Vermonters I know are in this book, but I've changed most of the names because they may not want to be portrayed as I see them.

Harold Taylor does not appear anywhere in it, under his own name or any other. And yet he was the inspiration for many of the traits I've since found and cherished in other Real Vermonters.

Harold Taylor would have been embarrassed, but very quietly pleased, to know that Vermont Seasonings *is dedicated to his indelible memory.*

Steve Delaney
Milton Vermont
July, 2007

CONTENTS

CONTENTS

viii

August

September

October

CONTENTS

X

Acknowledgments

A manuscript is born when you have an itch that becomes so strong that you have to scratch it.

A book is born when other people help you scratch it.

Vermont Seasonings emerges from the collaborative world of journalism. Early forms of some of the essays appeared first on Monitor Radio or as opinion pieces in *The Christian Science Monitor*. I'm grateful to David Cooke and Sue Schardt for shaping those efforts fifteen years ago, and to the *Monitor* for permission to use updated versions of those broadcasts and columns.

Other essays were first exposed a decade ago on Vermont Public Radio, which has also granted permission for their use.

At VPR Betty Smith edited and Brendan Walsh, Chris Albertine and Sam Sanders polished, and what emerged was better for their touch.

When the collection grew into "the idea that wants to be a book," I was buoyed up by Frank Dobisky and Cherryl Jensen, who offered encouragement, and by the steady support of Vermont poet Beth Kanell, especially in the doggerel sections.

Mike Donoghue of *The Burlington Free Press* was instrumental in moving the manuscript toward publication.

I want to thanks George Geers at Plaidswede Press for believing, and Sid Hall at Hobblebush Books for his craftsmanship.

And most of all, Lynn Delaney, editor of *The Milton Independent* and of my life, has inspired or constrained me, as needed.

INTRODUCTION

Reflections on the Rhythms of a Vermont Year

It's five thirty in the morning, and eighteen degrees below zero. The headlights pick out a light flurry of little white balls that would be snowflakes if it were warmer.

The bitter cold is sucking a last trace of moisture out of the January sky, where a moon just after full hovers before setting, veiled by the diamond dust. That's what Vermonters call this kind of snowfall, especially when an early sun glints off a coating of it. Meteorologists call it ice crystals. That's a concession to scientific terminology, which is an occupational disease among weather-mongers.

Vermont is a great place to practice the inexact science of weather forecasting. That's because we're poised almost exactly halfway between the Equator and the North Pole, and so we have four distinct seasons.

They don't follow the calendar precisely, and that may help explain why the forecasting is a bit haphazard. When you wake up to find several inches of "partly cloudy" on the ground in October, it's clear that winter doesn't wait for the December Solstice. And in northern Vermont, spring doesn't really get going until the leaves appear in May.

But the seasons are serially unique, and even though three of them are compressed to allow for a five-month winter, Vermonters cherish each in its turn. They are so distinctive that each one ushers in activities that occur only at that time of the year.

Within the seasonal framework, there are more subtle shifts in the air and earth around us, and in the waters as well.

The essays that follow are an attempt to capture those changes as Vermont rotates through the stately cycle of the four seasons and their infinite variations.

This is not an original idea, and it's not even confined to words.

Antonio Vivaldi captured the four seasons in music almost three hundred years ago and, ever since, other musicians, poets and choreographers have mined the same theme.

What is it that provokes artist after artist to search for new ways to react to the same cycle of greening and growth, of ripening and repose?

The answer may be buried deep in our cultural imprints. For as long as we've been aware of the difference between rain and shine, we've also known that we react differently to them.

In short, the seasons move us, and occasionally we feel compelled to say so.

GLOSSARY

Vermont-Speak Glossary

Vermonters speak American English, almost. Some words and terms have their own meanings here:

Away (n): All parts of North America except *Vermont*. *Away* is not divided into particular places. It is enough to note that it's not *Vermont*.

Down-country (n): *Away*, but less dismissive.

Flatlander (n): Person from *Away*. The term is often used to shrug off inexplicable behavior in a stranger.

R. F.: (see below)

Recovering Flatlander (n): Person from *Away* who has moved to *Vermont* and who believes it may be possible to pass as a *Real Vermonter*. It's not.

Vermont (n): Rumpled back corner of New England, where Old America lingers, as Old Ireland lingers in that country's western counties.

Vermonter (n): Person who lives in *Vermont*. *Vermonter* is subject to modifying adjectives.

R. V.: (see below)

Real Vermonter (n): (*Loose definition*) Person who has always lived in *Vermont*.

Real Vermonter (n): (*Strict definition*) Person who has always lived in *Vermont*, and whose parents have always lived in *Vermont*.

Real Vermonter (n): (*Ultra-Orthodox definition*) Person who has always lived in *Vermont*, whose parents have always lived in *Vermont*, and whose ancestors have always lived in *Vermont*, for at least seven generations. Occasionally insufferable about it.

VERMONT SEASONINGS

MARCH

The Elbows of the Year

A noun is a name, the name of a thing.
Call out that name, and envision its essence:

Ball: A small round globey thing that bounces.
Football: Round, but not completely so. Has elbows like a year.

A year has elbows, sure it does.
It's round but not completely so,

Slightly curved at wintertop and summerbottom,
Sharply bent at the elbows of September and March.

The sun moves north and brings more day than dark in March.
September is the blush of trees soon to go naked into winter.

At solstice top and bottom, the pass of seasons is mostly promise.
The pace of change is quicker at the elbows of the year.

Election Day

The Board of Civil Authority runs elections in my town, and as a new board member (you get there by being elected a Justice of the Peace) I've just helped to conduct my first election.

In Milton we don't have an old-fashioned Town Meeting any more. Rather, the town and school officials hold an information meeting the night before (it's poorly attended) and lay out what's in their budgets, and in any other ballot article someone asks about. And the next day, the voters troop in to make their marks on the ballots.

When there are high clouds at dawn, there's often a moment when they take on a pink tinge, even though the sun that's lighting them can't be seen.

If that happens in early March it occurs between six and six thirty.

That's when I turn up at Town Hall, armed with a cup of coffee and only a vague understanding of what to do. Fortunately the official duties are light, the Town Clerk and his staff are very efficient, and my colleagues on the Civil Board have forgotten how many times they've done this.

I'm the only new election official, and while I'm closing in on retirement age, I'm way younger than the rest of the board. They all seem to know the older voters, the ones who have stayed on the farm or in the village, the ones whose children live in Ohio and Texas and New York and Virginia, and bring their children to visit in the summertime.

The election officials like it when voters bring their kids to the polling place. They say it teaches them respect for the institutions of democracy. I think maybe those voters are having child-care problems, but I don't say so. After all, I'm an apprentice, here to learn the ropes.

The first thing I notice is how many of the voters are older than I am, and how many of them are people I haven't gotten to know in the fifteen years I've lived here. It's well known that older people are faithful voters, but I now think it's not just tax rates and campaign promises that bring them out.

To the older voters, my election official teammates are old pals, friends of a lifetime they may not have seen since the last election.

The voters move slowly past a table staffed by sprightly grandmas.

One tells them to sign in, and to pronounce their names out loud, even if the clerk has known that name for seventy years. It's part of the Election Day ritual. One finds their names on the Grand List of voters, and makes a neat checkmark. One hands out pencils, and one handles the ballots. She's been doing that for 37 years, and has curly white hair and the traces of an Irish accent. "You'll be fillin' out both sides now," she chirps.

The line moves slowly because the ladies also extract other information from the passing voters.

"I haven't seen your mother today," prompts the pencil clerk. Mother isn't well, and is voting absentee. Pictures of grandchildren are shared, and stories of sons who married girls from Away and then moved there.

The fabric of the community is being knitted together, both here and at the other end of the voting process, where the men cluster around the ballot box.

The voters come out from behind the striped curtains

of the booths, with their marked ballots held so no one
can see what they've done. They slide them into the slot
with great care.

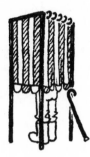

Many of them wear heavy boots and green denims
and have the huge hands and heavy shoulders of dairy
farmers. These voters all stop and ask an election officer
whose opinion they value, "How's your sugar?"

In the part of America that's known here as Away,
that question might refer to a girlfriend or even a wife.
Here it's about the season's first crop, and the answer
will solidify the asker's judgment of the maple sap run
in this year's early spring.

"Well, we've made 256 gallons, most of it fancy, but
last year we made 274." They agree that sugar seasons
have been oddly irregular in recent years. They dredge
up old memories of teams of horses who could pull a
collection sled through a sugarbush and stop at each
bucketed tree without being told.

And they ridicule the newly issued Vermont quarter, the one that shows a farmer collecting sap from
two maple trees. They say the artist was a Flatlander,
because any Real Vermonter knows a real sugarmaker
would never go into the trees wearing a flowing scarf,
an item they think is most un-Vermont. But one man is
saving those quarters for a grandson who lives Down-
country. That's another name for Away.

They do not talk about the issues on the ballots they
have just cast, and they most certainly do not say how
they voted. Further, they think it's rude to ask. Instead,
they pause for a few minutes to buff up old friendships.

They polish the legends of town characters who were
old when they were young. They talk about syrup prices
(could be better) and about hiring good help (they don't
know how to work any more). Then they move stiffly

out of the hall. *They* know how to work, these old men, and it shows in what those decades of labor have done to their bodies.

Many of them now use canes, and in a few more years they'll be gone, taking with them a culture that still defines the rural parts of Vermont.

My generation is about to replace them, but we were steeled in crucibles far different from the Great Depression and World War Two; forces that shaped the old men who come in to vote and to gossip on Election Day. Were we toughened and tempered enough in our turn to become the next keepers of the "Vermont state of mind"?

And will Election Day still function as the site for rekindling old friendships and remembering absent companions?

We won't know until the next generation begins to say of us, "Those old men knew how to work." Or will they?

If such values are still intact in the villages of Vermont, maybe it's because the old men and the old ladies have kept them for us. Can this generation capture and retain those civic virtues, and will the next one notice, or care?

My friend the sugarmaker worries about that. He's afraid that loosening the rules on absentee ballots and the new trend toward computer voting will remove something vital from the life of small towns; their traditional elections. And now I worry about that too.

Does that mean my apprenticeship is over?

Birches and Bending

Birch trees still bend, just as they did a century ago when Robert Frost dreamed of his young boy swinging on them.

When I first met Robert Frost in an anthology of American poets considered safe for school children, I lived in a place where birches don't grow. I was of an age when I thought the most important thing about birches was that clever Indians used to make canoes from strips of their bark.

But then a teacher made me read what Robert Frost thought was special about birches.

> . . . *birches bending left and right*
> *across the lines of straighter, darker trees . . .*

The idea of swinging on a tree that would be kind enough to bend and set me down again after a free ride was enough to fuel the imagination, and so I became a fan of birches.

It was an introduction to the idea that trees have differences beyond the distinction between needles and broad leaves. Especially in the northern forest that covers the northeastern corner of this country, you can see many of them side by side. Maples are sweet, oaks are sturdy, hickories are tough, beeches are bear-food, cedars are shingles and birches are the neighborhood rowdies.

This season the birches have bent under the weight of ice that sparkles so in the sunlight that it's easy to see why the makers of slang decided to call diamonds "ice."

9

They'll stay bent for a while, and then under the influence of sap and sunlight, they'll straighten, but only so far. Ice does indeed leave a permanent mark. Sometimes the trees bend over so far they look as if their trunks are made of rubber, and those never thrive.

But even where they grow ice-free, you'll seldom see a straight birch.

They are not good soldiers in the regiment of trees in the northern forest. There's too much Vermont in them, too much self-conscious casual. It's almost as if their stance, never quite vertical, is deliberate. Maybe it's a pose put on to annoy the spruce, which of course stand at rigid attention. In fact there's something about the slouchy posture of a clump of white-clad birches that suggests a set of sailors on leave in a tropical port. Any stance that's vaguely vertical will do.

Do you suppose that poplars are really birches that have had to turn in their uniforms and leave the family for the sin of standing too straight?

Maybe Robert Frost had it wrong after all. Maybe birches bend simply because they are non-conformist, casual and resistant to instruction by other trees as to how they should take care of their own business. When viewed from that angle, what good Vermonters birches make. And how dull the winter woods would be without their slashes of bright white across the somber shades of other trunks.

One could do worse than be a swinger of birches, Frost concluded.

Worse would be to be so poor of spirit as to miss noticing that birches are for uplift, whether for a young body or an old mind.

St. Patrick's Day

We have just passed the middle of one of the year's least charming months. A bad day for Julius Caesar, who was told to beware, and didn't. Once upon a time the Ides of March was a bad day for taxpayers too, until the tax code got so knotted up that they had to put off the day of reckoning by a month.

Now the Ides is a day of anticipation, because it ushers in St. Patrick's Day, which is set in the middle of March to atone for the rest of it. Shop owners and self-consciously Irish Irish-Americans green up their turf. Shamrocks abound, and so do the atrociously syrupy lyrics of seasonal tunes, some of them written by men who had not only never seen Ireland but had no drop of the Irish in them.

Hearing an Irish tenor melt down over lost lasses and lost lands and the virtues of ancient mothers, is enough to make you laugh out loud if you're sober, and burst into tears if you're not. Check out the words to Mother Machree some time. It's the verbal equivalent of sniffing gardenias.

A little whiff of sweetness is enough.

Now, I could get in trouble for picking on sentimental Irish music this week, if I were a Gonzalez or an Ishimaru or a Petrovsky. But as a Delaney I get a little wiggle room on issues of treason and heresy.

And speaking of heresy, it's a nice story about St. Patrick driving the snakes out of Ireland, but the sad truth is, there never were any snakes in Ireland. In fact the only lowly critter native to the Ould Sod is a newt.

11

Newts apparently cannot be banished by prayer, as Washington Democrats can attest. They may duck out of sight for a while, but they don't go away. The newts of Ireland are still there, too.

So are the English, especially in the north, and much of Irish history, both real and revisionist, is the story of the age-old struggle between English Empire and Emerald Island. As the headlines reflect all too often, that struggle ebbs and flows, but it does continue.

What is astonishing is that the English language, imposed by the British as a tool for breaking the Irish culture, has become a vehicle for Irish supremacy. Weaving the craft of the ancient Celtic bards into the new tongue, writers from Swift through Shaw and Wilde and Yeats and Joyce to Brendan Behan and Conor Cruise O'Brien have used the English language as a whip to smite the English.

Maybe the gift of gab, or the Blarney touch, or whatever it is that gives so many Irishmen a surgical skill with words, comes from old genetic and cultural sources. Maybe it's the inherent music and lilt of the Irish language that flavors the English of the Irish.

The Irish language is now in vigorous revival. Here's a well-known example, with its English translation:

Go n-eiri an botharleat
May the road rise up to meet you

Go raibh an choir ghaoithe gconai leat.
May the wind be always at your back.

Gi dtaitni an ghrian go bog blath ar do chlar eadiain,
May the sun shine warm upon your face,

Go gcuire an bhaisteach go bog min ar so ghort.
The rain fall soft upon your fields.

Agus go gcasfar le cheile sinn aris
And until we meet again

Go gcoinni Diai mbosa laimhe thu.
May God hold you in the palm of his hand.

"May the rains fall soft upon your fields." It's the images that make the words sing, in either language. And the words carry the baggage when it comes to moving an idea from one mind to another.

"If I don't get the words right," said a man who once ran the BBC World Service, "who will trust me with the ideas those words contain?"

We have hundreds of thousands of words, and the language is rich in ways to combine them into new ideas. Or ideas better stated.

Doing that might be a useful and quiet way to mark this St. Patrick's Day. Mine the language for nuggets of expression that lie there unexposed.

You might say, for example, that dreaming is an impractical exercise that yields nothing tangible, and that it takes hard work to turn expectations into reality.

Or you might say, "Dreams are of the heart, but deeds are of the hand."

That comes from a half-Irish, half-French author whose many Western novels tried to teach a generation of American boys the virtues of self-reliance. It's appropriate to cite Louis L'Amour during such an Irish-flavored week, in a place where so many surnames are French.

And may the rains fall softly upon your fields too, mon ami.

On the Road Too Long

Willie Nelson sang wistfully of being on the road again, outbound for adventure. John Denver sang longingly of the country roads that would take him home again.

The avenue away and the highway home are the same road. It just looks different from opposite ends. For years the road that connected home and away for me has been Interstate 89. The away lane leads to Boston and the road home ends in Milton, Vermont.

I've been over that road so many times that you could pull a blindfold off my eyes at any point along the way, and I can tell you the number of the next mile marker. I know the place in New Hampshire where a poplar sapling gets entombed every winter in the blue-white beard of frozen seepage from a rock wall on the roadside. That's at mile 38.

And one of my favorite spots is northbound near Brookfield, Vermont. There's a good-sized hill on the left, where a half-dozen tall white pines break the distant smooth outline of hardwood twigs against the sky.

To the road-weary eye those pines look like so many Comanche scouts on the skyline, checking out the wagon train on the trail below.

Yeah, I know, I've been on the road too long.

I keep looking for the small signs of change along the highway. For the end of bare branches and white ground that make the late winter seem to linger so. Old Vermonters believe that March brings a low point in the human reservoir of vitality, that our élan is at last

14

drained by the long winters. If they can make it through March, the old-timers claim, they'll be all right for the rest of the year. I'm not sure there are statistics to back up that notion, but it's a comforting thought now that we have almost made it through another March. Still, the winter seems endless, and there's not much charm left in even the most photogenic of snowfalls, the ones with the big fluffy popcorn flakes that are so welcome when they occur in October.

How many times have I driven on this stretch of highway? What effect have those multiple passages had on me?

It's easy to see the effect on the roadway. The pavement is cracking and breaking up, with an assist from the freeze-and-thaw cycles that make northern road-building such a challenge. I can see what the damage is, and sooner or later, probably later, the state will put mechanical teeth to the failing asphalt, and grind it up. Then the paving trucks will come along, and dump their loads into the hopper of a truly ugly machine that lays down a black ribbon one lane wide, like some sort of mechanical spider. Things have to get pretty bad before the state will spend all the money it takes to upgrade the road, but then by March the frost heaves have made all the roads look bad.

In another month or so the frost will come out of the ground and the pavement will settle down somewhat.

And will I? How shall I cope with the internal equivalent of frost heaves and potholes. How do I measure the success of my own effort to make it through March, to feel the resurgence of my own life force, after five months of having it leached away by the winter?

I drive the road and I see skinny tree trunks sticking up out of the snow-covered hillsides. And the tired

traveler's mind turns that image into a vision of bad hair transplants on balding scalps. I know, I've been on the road too long.

But the little mind games keep me alert and calm. That's important when some twenty-something oaf with an "I'm-from-Away" license plate goes by doing eighty-something, and slings road yuck onto my windshield. It comforts me to think the troopers might be working this stretch of I-89 today. Maybe I'll see one of those Massachachos parked in front of a flashing blue light. Would it be an expression of road rage to toot and give the trooper a thumbs-up as I go by? What a tempting thought that is.

But as I drive I keep looking for those little signs of change, of the warming and awakening that ought to go with the longer days we're having now, and at last, the first sign.

The hillcrests, where the bare branches seem the thickest, are taking on that purple-gray haze that means the buds are swelling. All the other changes to come will cascade off that slight coloration along the ridge-tops.

Dormancy still dominates in this season before spring, and yet rebirth begins. The day outlasts the dark, and now it's sugarin' season. The earth begins to thaw, and maple roots begin to draw.

In the sugarbush wise old horses drag their sap sleds from tree to tree and stop where they should without being told, as young men empty pails of the season's first harvest. The clear sap flows downhill to sugarhouses where old men with patient hands and knowing eyes boil it into syrup, gold and amber brown.

Taste!

And start the cadence of the quickening, of Spring.

APRIL

Geoffrey Chaucer Ruined April

Whan that Apryll with his shoures soote . . .

Remember that, from English Lit?
Did Chaucer know that what he writ,
The most intimidating verse of note,
Would force us all to learn by rote?

While teachers tried to 'splain "y-clept"
I must confess that I y-slept.
We students fled such verbal twists,
Ran off to be economists.

I have a grudge against that wight;
His famous poem isn't right.
Because that's where we learned to say
That Apryll shoures bring floures in May.

That might be so in Merrie Olde
But in Vermont it's verrie colde.
And Spring is late and Apryll flodde
Brings only thaw and lots of Mudde.

The Fragrant Mists of Fairfield

The sap is running in the sugarbush and so the Busheys are in the woods turning tree juice into Vermont maple syrup, along with sugarmakers from all over northern New England. It's time.

You can't tap too early, you've got to tap at the right time, and then you've gotta be ready to work with Mother Nature.

Mother Nature and the Busheys of Fairfield, Vermont have been partners in maple sugaring for about 150 years. Marcel Bushey is the patriarch of one branch of a legendary sugaring family. They operate the old-fashioned way. Boil the sap down to syrup over a wood-fueled fire. No oil burners. Gather the sap in buckets and pour it into horse-drawn sledges. No tractors.

The horses seem to work out good. They don't disturb the soil or cause erosion or anything like that, so I guess there's a place for them.

Come on, girls!

There's a place for horses in Danny Bushey's heart. He's been sugaring behind Queenie and Blondie for more than a decade. Dragging that sledge is the only job Queenie and Blondie have, and before the season starts, the Busheys get them into shape by having them drag loads of concrete around the barnyard. After the season they'll go back to a soft life in the pastures, along with six other massive horses, some of them Belgians or Clydesdales. They all know a lot about sugaring, and they all stop their sledges when they get to the next bucket-laden tree, and they do it without being told.

18

Danny Bushey says Nature provides the sap, but the quantity and the quality depend on the spring weather, on a timely cycle of warm days and cool nights.

This past week has been an excellent week. We've got a good snow cover. And that helps the color, keeps the sap cool. It all works together. It's gotta stay cool. Right now it looks good. We're hopin' it lasts a few more weeks.

Once the buds begin to swell on their twigs, the sap turns bitter and the season is over. In the Bushey clan young men are in the woods from mid-morning to "can't see" time at night. Over Marcel Bushey's lifetime, that has taken a toll.

Well, the hills get steeper. The hills get steeper.

So old men are in the sugarhouse turning maple sap into Vermont gold. As Marcel Bushey explains, it takes about 35 gallons of sap and a lot of hard work to make one gallon of syrup.

Which president was it, I think it was Jefferson suggested that every state, every place that had the climate, the temperature, should produce maple syrup because it was something that wasn't produced by slave labor. But I kind of question that a little bit.

You've heard it said that old sugarmakers never die, they just evaporate. So that's what it amounts to. You just evaporate the water and have the goodies left.

Sounds very simple.

Yeah.

But there's an art to it?

Oh my, yes, there's a big art to it. My gosh, there's a . . . I mean some people can stand right there and look at the pan and see it burn and not know what's going on, and what's the art is to be able to anticipate that so you don't get to that crisis.

Sugarmaking keeps Vermont farmers busy in the season between seasons, but the Busheys are more involved than most. It takes a thousand gallons of sap to produce a thirty-three gallon barrel of syrup. The Busheys produce about six barrels a day, each worth about eight hundred dollars.

But if you ask about money, a cloud comes over the old sugarmaker's sunny face, and you can tell he thinks the question is none of your business. Suddenly the canny Yankee is sitting where the chuckling storyteller was a moment ago.

Well, if you have a good year, you might buy a piece of equipment, and if you have a bad year, why, you break even.

He doesn't say that the "piece of equipment" is probably a new baler or tractor, and the prices start somewhere above $50,000.

Are you having a good year, or are you having a bad year?

Well, uh, it's too early to tell. Too early to tell. Actually I'm optimistic. Um, to quote Yogi Berra, it ain't over till it's over.

Bushey has talked about easing up a bit, slowing down a little. But quitting is out of the question. Maple sap runs in Bushey veins, and there's a generation of grandchildren to teach about tapping and horses and boiling, all the family skills. After all, there's a tradition to keep up. A legacy of sugaring that's been a symbol of spring in the northern reaches of Vermont ever since the long-ago discovery of sweet sap.

Indians were first . . . supposedly one threw his tomahawk against a tree and it started bleeding, and the squaw caught the sap and cooked his meat in it, and he was a happy chief.

And so is Marcel Bushey, surrounded by his horses, his sons and the fragrant mists of his sugarhouse.

Better Late . . .

Yesterday I passed spring on the highway. It was moving north at about the speed of a butterfly near the town of Lebanon. That's about where the waistlines of New Hampshire and Vermont would be, if states had such things. U.S. Route 4 would be the belt.

I told my friends in northern Vermont that spring is on the way, but they were skeptical. They always are, which is good. Skepticism is a valuable trait in friends. It allows them to help you keep your head on straight.

But spring really is coming. Last week it was fluttering along down near the Massachusetts border, somewhere near U.S. Route 9, the Brattleboro-Bennington axis.

In our tiny state, it's convenient to use the main roads as regional dividers. When the weather guys want to say it's going to be warmer in southern Vermont, they say "south of Route 4." Weather trauma confined to the north is "north of Route 2." And when it's a northeast-southwest divide, I-89 marks the frontier between weathers. Or it's "East of the Greens."

Clearly the town of Milton where I live (north of Route 2, astraddle of I-89) is not a priority stop on spring's delivery schedule. Mother Nature does not use Fedex or UPS to put spring where it's wanted, until she's good and ready to put it there.

The extra waiting for spring that's required if you live in this country's northern marches is especially trying in this age of instant images.

There's TV coverage of the Masters' golf tournament, and the Augusta National course is buried in azaleas. TV shows us the cherry blossoms blooming brilliantly in Washington. My southern cousins call wickedly to say they're getting peas and asparagus out of their gardens. I say that's nice and hang up. Then I go outside and try to figure out which part of a slowly drying mudflat is my driveway, and which is supposed to be grass. I'll put my peas in some time in the middle of May, and the asparagus comes in June. So too, do my few struggling azaleas.

There have been what the ancients called signs and portents of spring. Lake Champlain's Inland Sea thawed one brisky day last week, and now the water is so high that the waves are using driftwood hammers to pound more beach out of what used to be grass along the lakeshore.

There's a seasonal mini-lake that forms in highwater years when the wave wash gets trapped in a low area near the dooryard of my neighbor's camp. We call it Lake Harry, and around its edges there's usually a tennis ball or two mixed in with the other floating debris.

Oh, and some geese have been seen, flying north through the snow flurries. There's a rumor that the temperature got up into the seventies in southern Vermont this week. But that's an unreliable portent because it's well known around here that southern Vermont is full of transplanted Bostonians and New Yorkers, who tend to overvalue warm weather.

There are other signs that the grip of winter is relaxing, and these are more reliable indicators. Maple sugar season has come and gone, and along with it the tedious process of cleaning up. One of my neighbors has fixed the flat tire on his tractor, the one that deflated back in November. He's going to need that tractor in another week or ten days.

So spring is still a week or so away around here. I will know when it gets here because it comes in with the impact of a thunderclap. Spring has waited so long to arrive that all its pent-up energy explodes in a burst of new life that seems packed into just a few days.

The crocuses croak and the forsythias syth and the blossoms bloss and finally the mud hardens. And all of a sudden it's May. That's Nature's month of Yes-you-May, and all the restraints are off as the greening of Vermont slips its leash and gambols across the softening landscape. Ash saplings put on two feet of sudden growth, dandelions are briefly a welcome sight and hayfields go from beige to emerald almost overnight.

But Mother Nature is a superb balancer, and the exuberant rush of spring brings with it a reminder that for every give-away there's a take-away.

Just when all the plus marks of spring make the days seem paradisical, she sends us blackflies, who are homicidical. Mother Nature is indeed a tough scorekeeper.

That Joyant Sucking Sound

In the years after the American Revolution, when settlers were pouring through the Cumberland Gap into Kentucky and the lands along the Ohio River, the northwest corner of New England was still largely unsettled.

And yet there are towns in northern Vermont that are over two hundred years old. Milton, the one I live in, was chartered in 1763, but not settled for another thirty years. My town has escaped going through quaint on its way to old.

And after more than two hundred years, much of the North Country is still sparsely settled, from Lake Champlain's Missisquoi Bay all the way across upper New Hampshire and the empty quarter of Maine to Houlton, where I-95 ends at the New Brunswick border crossing.

About 300 million people live in the United States, and two hundred ninety-nine and a half million of those people do not live in Vermont. Now, there's a lot to be said for that, but there are practical reasons as well why such a beautiful place is so thinly inhabited.

This month, one of those practical reasons is upon us, and it has been overwhelming. During the spring thaw, Vermont's name is mud.

Up here, when the frost goes out of the ground, you can invent entire new definitions for words like squishy. And you can invent new descriptions for mud. Some of them you can even say on the radio.

During a cold winter the frost line is about four feet

deep in the earth, and funeral homes stop conducting interment services because nobody can dig through it. Wintertime obituary notices contain the phrase "interment in the spring, at the convenience of the family."

There's a shrub called a serviceberry, and when it comes to life each year, the earth is warm enough for burial services to be held. That shrub also signals the arrival of mud season.

Mud season is not much of a problem where the soil is sandy, because water drains well through sand, and once the deep frost is gone, the earth settles down nicely. But of course all the roads are built where the soil is clay. Now, as any potter knows, clay is good at trapping water. The ceramics industry is built on that trait. Vermont road mud isn't in demand for making pottery, but it does have unique characteristics.

There are forty miles of dirt road in my town, and during mud season even the label "dirt" doesn't fit. Some of our roads have a consistency that an old Vermonter calls "P to Q." That is, somewhere between playdough and quicksand.

I live on one of those roads, and I drive on a lot of them. So every year I dread the day when I make my first phone call to Henry Lamoreaux.

Every year the call goes something like this:

Lamoreaux Towin' Service . . .

Hello Henry, it's Steve Delaney.

Sank yer Jeep again, did ya?

Yes, Henry.

Where'd ya lose it this toime?

On the Swamp Road. About a mile past where Wendell's sugarhouse used to be.

Oh, that's a baad spot. I make a livin' offa that road. They don't call it Swamp Road fer nothin', ya know.

25

Yes, Henry, you said that last year.

Oy did? Well you just set toight, and Oy'll be roight out ta get ya.

Don't sound so cheerful about it.

Why not? It's noice ta make a livin' doin' good deeds. Besides, pullin' out Jeeps is the most fun of all.

Why is that?

Well, Jeeps make the best joyant suckin' sound when the mud finally let's 'em go. That's cause the drivers always go the four-wheel and sink 'em in good.

I don't want to talk about that.

Well you just set toight, and Oy'll be roight out.

Every time Henry hears that giant sucking sound, somebody pays him twenty five dollars. And whoever said there is no joy in Mudville forgot to ask Henry Lamoreaux.

Lamoreaux Towin' Service . . . Oy can't come ta the phone roight now, the Hardscrabble Road just ate a little Geo, and Oy've gone out ta raise it.

Just leave a message and then set toight, and Oy'll be roight out ta get ya.

The Color of Life

In the middle of last month, we Irish-Americans had our annual spasm of greenness, asserting our identity by insisting, for a day, that traffic lines on roads and beer in kegs, should appear in the color that serves us as a tribal totem. Let's not get carried away, cousins. Green is also the color of the Islamic Jamahariyya of Libya, where Guinness is banned, to say nothing of Bushmill's, and where the landscape is mostly the beige of sand.

Political parties as well as nations have co-opted the color green as their own. In Western Europe there are vigorous Green factions whose members see issues through the emerald glasses of environmental activism.

Perhaps green should be apolitical. Maybe we simply shouldn't allow the color of life to be used as a partisan or sectarian symbol. Isn't it too important for that?

Look how anxiously we await the re-greening of Vermont after seven months of depending on the deep dull coats of evergreens for evidence that there is such a thing as chlorophyll. Look how avidly we tell each other of early sightings: the first grass-like leaf of a crocus, the confident thrust of daffodils and the stealthy coloring of lawns.

All that is tasty to the mind, of course, but like most appetizers, not quite satisfying.

We're waiting patiently through the preliminaries, anticipating the main event: the greening of the trees.

After all, it's only when the maples and oaks and poplars and their kin are fully clothed that we can claim

27

our title in full comfort: The Green Mountain State. In the fall our Green Mountains are multi-colored, and during the long winters they're gray-brown, except for the places where the birches live, and where the skiers play.

Now that's changing, and the weeping willows are a bit ahead of the pack, showing a vibrant yellow that's about to slide into green. But most of the others are busily packing life into buds that will soon be too tight to contain the annual explosion of leaves.

The grass is about to take off. By the third week in May it will be knee-high, and the mowers and balers will begin their stately spirals through the hayfields.

And by the second week in May my neighbor's house that's been visible through the empty spaces between tree trunks will disappear as those empty spaces fill with leaves in search of sunshine.

I've got nothing against lilacs and apple blossoms. In fact they appeal to more of my senses than the leaves do, but they too are preamble, scents wafting through the wilderness of pre-color, announcing the coming of the green, not its presence.

Almost everything on Earth owes its life to the annual greening of the plants. No wonder the ancients made the greening a festival. And no surprise that modern people who have retained a sense of wonder, like the Irish, embrace the color of life.

The Irish claim there are forty shades of green in their rainy little island. I wonder how many they could find here in the next month or so.

MAY

Heyjack Hawaya

He marches by, defining spry, with step made small by fear of fall.
He's fled his home, come out to roam, to grab a share of brisky air.

He's risking wrath to tread the path, for that inspires his daughter's ires.
"Beware the risk," she's prone to *tsk*, but his old heart still does its part,
And he's a fixture among the mixture of those who pack the asphalt track.

He tips his hat (was raised like that) and shyly greets each one he meets.
The magic is that as they whiz along on wheels or high-tech heels
They wave right back, "Hello there, Jack!"

Does he recall, when he was tall, an hour's run was just for fun?
Does he resent those legs now bent? If that be so, it doesn't show.
He totters on and I am drawn to wonder how on my own brow
I'll wear the years when it appears that I can't do what I used to.

I hope I can, like that old man, get out and walk and share some talk
With those who jog and those who slog, whose greetings say, for one more day,
"Hello there, Steve, you're still aleve!"

Green-Up Day

What I love about radio is the way it uses sound and suggestion to create images in the mind. They are often vivid images, especially when crafted to draw a response and stimulate action by the listener.

My mind can see you, tomorrow morning, and you're listening through headphones to a small radio clipped to your belt. That leaves your hands free for picking up the by-products of the packaging industry on Green-up Day.

Wrong image? You're not going to be prowling the ditches of some country road tomorrow morning, or prospecting a vacant lot for the season's first harvest, the fruits of other people's indifference?

Oh, I've got it. You'll be in the car, taking more trash bags to the Green-up volunteers scattered in teams along the roads of your town. No? Oh, too bad.

You'll be missing a great chance to vent some righteous indignation. I always get angry while walking the roadsides to retrieve the junk that people throw away. It's a great way to remind myself not to heave things I don't want out the car window. Look what's already there!

Tires, household garbage, used diapers, unlucky lottery tickets, drink containers; and why is it that the cans and bottles that hold *expensive* beer are never found along the roads?

And don't forget the car parts, motor oil containers, McFood wrappers, and the endless samples of unidentifiable mess left behind by the careless, the mindless, the

30

shiftless and the clueless. Every year I want to find one of those people and yell, "How could you do this?"

Green-up Day is a reason to feel good about doing good. It was invented in the first flush of the ecology movement, and it's been going strong ever since. The idea behind Green-up Day resonates with Vermonters, who take great pride in the physical beauty of the state, and in the fact that we banned billboards, and introduced a bottle return bill years ago, to keep our scenery looking scenic.

Green-up Day is well timed, in theory, to fall on the first Saturday in May.

The mud is gone and the grass hasn't yet covered the trash in the ditches with a new coat of greenery. But some years it seems the timing's a bit off. Either it's cold or it rains, or the blackflies are out early to prove in their own way that evil exists.

The remarkable thing is, people turn out anyway, in huge numbers. Many of them never step forward to do any other kind of community service. But on Green-up Day, there they are in boots and gloves, often with their kids, going out to teach by example. Almost five hundred people get their assignments from the coordinators at the town park, and then fan out, returning at the end of the morning for hot dogs and soda. The local paper takes pictures, and some kids get T-shirts, for winning a division of the unusual trash contest.

There's always a toilet seat, and there's always evidence that poachers stalk the deer when they're yarded up out of season in the deep snow of winter. And there's always some truly ugly "what is it?" that was probably identifiable when it was new, but not any more.

In Milton, where I live, a woman who makes teddy bears and a man who makes old houses new have run Green-up Day for years. They've made it the most

successful trash collection effort held anywhere in the county. Of course, in the snootier towns they say no wonder Milton collects so much trash. Look who lives there! It's hard to ignore that, but we try.

In the end thousands of tons of trash get bagged for the road crews to pick up, and the anger at those who litter turns into pride in a job well done.

Tell you what. Between now and tomorrow morning, find out where your town's Green-up team is working, and go volunteer. Or just get a plastic bag and walk a neglected roadside, even if you're a visitor. Especially if you're from Away. The experience will teach you a lot about what makes people tick in the back corner of New England.

And by the way, you really don't need the T-shirt. The Green-up medal is the one you wear inside, where you keep your most important trophies.

. . . and One Step Back."

When a toddler throws tantrums and forgets what the toilet is for, it's called regression, and it's often triggered by the arrival of a new baby in the household.

When a month like May turns itself inside out and starts acting like March, that's regression too, and we try to figure out why we're in the outhouse of the weather gods. Our best answer: "It happens."

It happened this week.

The grass has been greening up for a couple of weeks now, and this week it's spangled with the bright yellow of dandelion blossoms. And on top of that there's a dusting of snow. White on green on gold.

White and gold are the colors of the Papacy and of the flag of the Vatican. Green is the color of Ireland.

This morning my dooryard wears all three colors. Imagine an Irish Papacy. Well, we've already had a Polish one.

After all, the odd-colored lawn is proof that improbable things can happen.

There's a ring of ice around the edges of the pond. The sun will destroy it in an hour or so in an effort to restore the normal order of things. Do you suppose that the sun is embarrassed? After all, it's only six weeks away from its high point in the sky, and ice is now supposed to be a memory. And yet the signs of spring look oddly fragile and tentative amid a light coating of snow.

It's heartening that the snow looked tentative as well. There wasn't much of it, and most of what fell came down in slow motion, in one of those photogenic spates

of big fat flakes that just don't have that serious indus-
trial-strength blizzard look of the snows of deep winter,
when the flakes are smaller and slam into the ground
with the clear intention of obliterating all details of the
bare earth. But fluffy or not, this snowfall happened in
May.

Oh yes, things are not as they should be. We don't
want March intruding into the second week in May. It
often does, but we find it easy to forget those incur-
sions, as if they were annoying quirks in the behavior
of a favorite relative. Incurable; but endurable.

So we endure. More, we gape at the oxymoron: snow
on dandelion flowers! How unusual is that! Well, not
very. In Vermont's northern mountains it snows a little
in May every year and in the Champlain Valley, where
I live, every three years or so. And while the cold is
unpleasant and unwelcome after a cold winter and an
intoxicating taste of spring warmth, it does have its good
points.

Maybe the cold will kill the blackflies! What a boon
that would be.

Blackflies are about an eighth of an inch long, and
about half as wide, and about as welcome as a rabid
rat. You're likely to be bitten anywhere outdoors while
they're in season. But if you're in or near the woods,
and if you sweat, just a little, the odds go up. You never
feel the bite, but pretty soon there's a light itch, and you
slap it, creating a bloody little splat where the fly had
been feeding. And then the swelling and the real itching
begin. You can get a welt the size of a quarter in no time
at all, and they love to attack the tight points. When I'm
wearing Hat IV, the one with the faded Red Sox "B" on
the front, the little pests strike where the hat meets my
forehead. Hat IV?

That's the great-grandson of Hat, the one I wore

in the Sinai desert until it blew off an armored car in a sandstorm. Hat II was eaten by a malevolent washing machine, and Hat III is in honorable, tattered retirement.

Maybe the cold will ease by tomorrow. Tomorrow there's an interment service for old Mr. Cashman, who died in January. As I've said, you can't bury people in January in Vermont, you have to wait for the thaw. I think it'll be all right. The serviceberries are out, and it's possible to dig again. But for the family's sake I hope it's warmer.

After all, this can't last long, this retrograde weather. It's an expression of nature, a last blast of arctic air sweeping down out of Hudson's Bay, and it must give way to the growing warmth in the Northern Hemisphere. The cold is a natural occurrence, but way untimely.

We were going to put in the peas this week. Now maybe we'll wait a few days.

There's a reason why things are not done out of season, and RVs seldom get caught pushing the season.

This week is proof that my neighbor is right in refusing to turn on the water in a string of lakeside camps he owns, until May 15th. Real Vermonters have learned over the decades that while anomalies in the weather are rare enough to stand out, they are also common enough to take note of, in deciding when it's time to take two steps forward.

Showtime at Sunrise

The gifts of spring have arrived in northern Vermont, somewhat late but all the more welcome. Among them is a large log pushed up on the beach in the last convulsion of winter. Loose ice and a lot of other stuff goes migrating on the wind during ice-break on Lake Champlain.

This log has been around. The bark is gone and one of the ends is hollow. The other end may have been shaped by the chisels of beaver teeth. It was probably a poplar or a cottonwood, one of those soft hardwoods, but I can't tell which.

The early sun lights up Whiteface, the skiers' Olympic mountain forty miles west, near Lake Placid. From here it's the dominant peak in the Adirondack skyline. That's because Mount Marcy is so much farther away, a little blue triangle poking into the edge of the sky.

The white face of Whiteface glows in the nearer distance and hogs the horizon. It's compelling, a star of the skyline that sucks up my attention the way a black hole draws gravity and light.

I should be thinking about serious things, but when I'm being a bump on that battered old log, it's hard to grapple with notions like why kids grow up cynical, and why politicians abandon competence.

Instead I watch the gray of dawn ripen into Technicolor along the West Coast of New England. Besides, there's a terrific show going on.

Robins are not the only early birds. Mama Merganser has her flotilla of little ducklings out for their morning diving and water-walking lessons. I think there are ten of them this year, but it's hard to count because some of them always seem to be underwater as the family swims along parallel to the shoreline.

When Mama calls, they all get up and run across the water, legs churning, water flying everywhere as they test wings that still have no lift. As a survival trait their dash is effective; as showbiz it's spectacular. None of the little ones says no when Mama says go. How refreshing.

The great blue heron goes by, using her broad wings as oars in the air, long neck tucked in and long legs straight back. She is teaching a smaller version of herself to stand so still at the water's edge that fish will think her legs are twigs, and swim near them.

This morning the heron sails over to the raft I've put out for the kids. Her approach reminds a dozen seagulls that they have errands to run and they scatter, leaving behind another layer of proof that they feed well.

In flight or in repose, the blue heron looks majestic. You could say the same thing about the gulls, at least in flight. *You* could but I won't, even though their sad cries define this place as much as the hiss and crunch of wavelets.

You are what you eat, say the nutritionists, and apart from the considerable grace of their flight, gulls are garbage. They've been described justly as rats with wings. They are greedy and quarrelsome and they steal food from each other's beaks. They remind me of the sort of people I don't invite to this beach paved in skipping stones, this place where I heal the marks left by the human gulls that inhabit the ordinary parts of my life. I pretend that hours spent here are not deducted from my lifespan, and may even extend it.

The barn swallows also fly brilliantly, but they don't understand real estate. This is *my* camp, my refuge. The swallows have the notion that I cannot come anywhere near the front door, because they have a nest under the awning above it.

I think barn swallows must have taught the finer points of dive-bombing to World War II pilots.

I don't mind their nest, but I refuse to be evicted for the sake of babies so ugly they stretch the limits of parental devotion. Whatever it is that makes puppies and kittens appealing got left out of the swallow gene pool.

The next time I sit here watching the morning mature I will try to figure out why the best fliers among the birds tend to have the worst manners. This time, I'm wondering if I'll ever hear the loons again without thinking of Katherine Hepburn and Henry Fonda. There was one out there last night.

You see, there are priorities, and they are different here. The order of things to worry about is determined by cool air and lapping waves and birdsong, and light so new it is still yellowed by the sunrise.

I will think about why war is popular, and why there is so much slaughter in the name of religion. All that in due course.

But not now, and certainly not here.

The Knot in the Pine

A Flatlander, even a self-professed Recovering Flatlander, is still a person from Away. We try to hide it, those of us who plan to live in Vermont from now on, but the evidence slips out despite all our efforts.

A Flatlander is the knot in the pine, and no matter how you try to paint over it, that knot will not stay hidden.

Neither will the evidence of Flatlanderhood. Here it is, although it hurts a lot to admit this.

Machinery hates me.

RVs understand machinery. A Real Vermonter can coax life out of any internal combustion engine with a tug or two, no matter how long it's been sitting idle. There must be some unspoken understanding between Vermotor and Verman, something that simply eludes Flatman.

Try as I might to conceal the flaw, there are two times during the year when it becomes obvious that I cannot master the machinery of convenience.

When we get the first heavy snow, usually in November, I'm out there with a shovel heaving away at the drifts across the driveway. RVs simply start their snowblowers and toss it aside. The motor clatters away happily, the augur churns and a great plume of snow sails away.

I have a snowblower too. Mine simply won't start, not for me. The guy whose wife works at the newspaper, and the guy who fixes small motors, even my wife, can start the damned thing. Not me. The small motor fixer laughs loudly when we demonstrate that Shiny Boots can, I can't. She's a Flatlander too, to make it worse. I go through the same motions but it doesn't work. So I shovel, and brood.

The other time machinophobia strikes is in May. Now, in the time of the daffodils.

I've got to mow the grass. It's growing clumpy and tall. Everybody else has pulled that starting rope, and gets rewarded for it when the motor runs and the blades turn. Not me. Everybody else has a neatly trimmed lawn with neat and concentric swath-lines, miniature versions of the mowing patterns that will turn pastures into abstract art next month during the first cutting of hay.

I try to deal with the problem by taking the mowers, the riding one and the walking one, for service in April.

When I pick them up, the mower man, an RV of course, starts them and they run beautifully. While I'm still there, I pull the ropes too, and they run beautifully.

At home, out in the yard, they don't. The mower man comes to the house, and looks strangely at me. He pulls the rope and the damned motor actually purrs. I say it must be me. He says he's never heard of such a thing and goes off to tell his friends over a beer or two.

I've got this customer, he says, who can't get a motor to run for him.

Must be a Flatlander, they say.

They all know.

There's small comfort in knowing it's a geo-genetic condition. I can't operate a small motor because I wasn't born here. That's all there is to it, and I suppose I could get used to that if it weren't such an obvious fault line between me and Real Vermonters.

It's not as if I get teased about it. RVs aren't cruel.

But teasing would be better then the looks of pity I get, the looks that they usually save for an old pet that needs to be put down.

There's a ditch the mower can't reach, and it's right out front where everybody can see it. I have to keep the weeds down in that ditch or people will think I'm a slob.

That's what trimmers are for. The small motor fixer has a dozen different kinds in his shop, and he assured me that any of them would do the job for me. "They're all reliable," he said.

Right. Hah. I know better. I won't buy one of those.

I do have a trimmer now, and it keeps that ditch clean, if I don't try to do too much at once. You see, it's battery powered, and it's humiliating to stand out there in plain sight, trying to make that under-powered trimmer look and act like the real thing. It's a bit like using a moustache trimmer to shear sheep.

People I know go by and honk. I'd like to think they do that just because they recognize me standing in that ditch and want to say hello.

But I know better. They honk because they want me to know they've seen me using that wimpy trimmer because a real one, with a gasoline motor, will not obey me.

It's like this every year, beginning in the middle of May. And don't even mention computers.

Remembering on Memorial Day

In a couple of hours, I will take some flowers to a cemetery in Milton and place them on my aunt's grave, alongside the World War II service medallion that holds a new American flag. She was an army nurse during the campaign in the Pacific islands.

But I'm going because she was my aunt, not because she was a captain in the U.S. Army Reserve.

When I was growing up, Memorial Day was more about family than it is now. Armistice Day, now Veterans Day, was more about soldiers and sailors who had laid down their lives or had come home to honorable discharges.

The State of Vermont has just lost one of its distinctions, and it involves Memorial Day. We were the last state to mark the occasion on its real date, May 30th. No more. Now it's the nearest convenient Monday, just like Presidents' Day and Martin Luther King Jr.'s birthday. I'm old enough and crotchety enough to resent that. Why should we lose track of the real dates of events important enough to memorialize, just to provide another convenient three-day weekend.

I remember a time and a place in which Memorial Day was just as solidly set in the calendar as July 4th or Christmas.

Out in the middle of Illinois, in Tazewell County where I once lived, there is a little cemetery fenced off between a field where the corn should be two or three inches high by now, and another field where the hay baler probably roared last week.

Harry and Thornton Mooberry were brothers in their sixties. They owned adjoining dairy farms, and on Memorial Day there would be no cultivating and no haymaking. The men and boys in their families would go and clean up the cemetery, and I would go with them as hired help, because in those days the family was a bit short of boys old enough to help and young enough to live at home.

The Mooberrys on that land went back to the 1830s when Abner, the first one, arrived from Pennsylvania. He's there, first row, left side. The family always did things in an orderly way. All of the headstones were modest, giving only the names and dates, no slogans, no carved angels. They were Mennonites, and plainness was bred into them, even though they weren't black-suit-no-machine Mennonites.

The thing that sticks in the mind after half a century is how proud those old men were of their elders. Both Harry and Thornton were short, compact men with the huge tough hands of dairy farmers. They did most of their chores in silence, but as they worked at trimming the grass and straightening up the stones, they told stories about how the land they loved had been cleared and tamed, about the Mooberry who shot the last bear, and the one who crashed his brand-new automobile into the Methodist church because he hadn't learned how to stop it. The stories just bubbled up, part reminiscence and part parable for the instruction of the young.

And if you had a question, you'd better ask while Harry and Thornton were still at work in the cemetery. If you asked later the answer would be, "That? Just a story, not important. You finish muckin' out after the hogs?"

But as they talked on those Memorial Days the personalities of Henry, 1866–1911, and George, 1848–1902, and a dozen others, began to emerge, just as their headstones became visible in the grass.

Harold Mooberry owns that land now. He inherited Thornton's farm and bought Harry's from sons who moved to cities, and a daughter who married into the Air Force. I wonder if Harold still looks after the graves on Memorial Day, including Harry's and Thornton's. I wonder if honoring the elders is still a part of bonding that family to their land, and I wonder if they still hire kids to help. After all, by now there are more stories to learn from.

There's a quiet little cemetery on a dirt road not far from my house. It's surrounded by a low stone wall, and there's some space left at the back.

Most of the folks who lie here are from old Vermont farm families, and have been here a long time.

Many of their surnames still ring in the community, in the rosters of high school sports teams, in the list of those who have served on the Board of Selectmen, and occasionally, in the police reports.

Others have been sort of isolated out here, with their descendants either moved on to places like the Mooberry farm in the Midwest, or simply married into other clans in an absence of sons.

The markers are modest, and the trees are huge. Everyone says trees grow best over a boneyard. Maybe they do.

I think I'd like to rest here when my time comes, and I know I'd like the folks who bear my name to come by once in a while and clear away the weeds.

Will I have to suggest that, or will they just know?

JUNE

Schools Don't Close for Haymaking Any More

Wind brings the bellow of the baler,
    the cadence of haymaking down by the stream.
        It strums a youthful ear and emerges as a grin.

The McLemores are making hay and classes soon will end.
    They're always first, the McLemores,
        their bottom-grass grows fast.

Many hands are needed now, and boys must do their share.
    The piston drives to pack the bale, the motor revs again.
        The summer is a'comin' now, its herald does proclaim.

Where now, those sturdy men who bound that hay?
    And where the dusty old machine that's long since had its day?
        Half a lifetime gone and more, they do it different now.

No more the wagon high with hay bales stacked like bricks.
    It's rolls, not bales, and one man does it all.
        From mow to stow, no need for many hands.

The kids don't hear that bellow now, the roller doesn't roar.
    Nor do they know technology has stripped their summer
        of the first three weeks in June.

Elegy for a Season

Spring blew through here like an Amtrak special, with a hint of its coming, a blast of its presence, and an echo of its passage.

It's over.

There are plenty of ways to tell when spring slides into summer.

Here are a few of the northern Vermont signs. They may not be as reliable or as date-certain as the portents the weather people use to predict what the wind and rain will do, but the sequence is right, and they are all signs of transition.

Remember when dandelions looked alluring? When they spangled newly greened pastures with their bright yellow flowers? That was in the spring, before they threw up those gray puffballs that carry their next generation onto your lawn. When that happens spring is over.

Do you recall seeing the fields tan and brown in their newly plowed nakedness? You can't see that any more. They've got rows of green stuff growing up out of them, striving to be knee high by the Fourth of July, and later as high as an elephant's eye. When the corn comes up, spring is over.

Were you watching when the ponds and lakes melted, and then rose as the ground thawed and the snowmelt ran off? That was in the spring. Now some of those ponds have kids in them. Of course kids have no thermostats, so they don't know the water is still too cold for swimming. But all that splashing is a sign that spring is over.

In some of the other fields you can see mechanized unicorns lumbering around, as tractors with one tusk spear the huge rolls of hay from the year's first cutting, and hoist them onto wagons. You can see them being hauled away to stand in ready rows near somebody's hungry Holsteins. When the fields take on that lime-green color that follows the first mowing, it isn't spring any more.

When I was a kid all that was understood. School and spring ended when June came. School and fall began when September did. All the time in between was summer.

I know the weather people say we've still got a couple of weeks before the summer officially arrives. The skywatchers anticipate the longest day, and the shortest night, and the farthest north the sun seems to get, and they say, "Not yet!"

There are still nights when the frost warnings are posted, and days when the north wind blows bitterly down from Canada. Sweaters are not yet allowed to hibernate.

Okay, then, not yet. But what about the other evidence? What about sightings of bumblebees, and the furious turf wars of barn swallows, and the emergence of caterpillars and fireflies and sailboats?

Those things don't happen in a vacuum; they're part of a pattern, and the pattern is one of transition.

Spring has sprung. It's always quick in Vermont, but this year it seems to have been compressed even more tightly than usual into just a few weeks, and now it's gone. The first half masquerades as winter and the last half pretends to be summer. There's hardly any room in between for apple blossoms.

To every thing there is a season, the old wisdom says, and a time to every purpose under heaven. Well, the purpose of the season of spring is to promise summer, and having delivered early upon that promise, to fall out of sight like the petals from a tulip past its time. And what's left, as the Gershwins understood, is summertime, and oh, so briefly in Vermont, the livin' is easy.

The Snowbird Inversion

You'd think that by the time the last sunshine of May warms the land, by the time the first hay cutting is rolled or cubed or chopped into sileage, and the asparagus comes up; you'd think by then that life in Vermont would be so benign there'd be nothing to complain about.

The cold has relented except for an occasional brisky night, and the mud has dried. My apple trees and my azaleas have gone in and out of bloom, and the grass grows loudly. In northern Vermont, you *can* hear it.

Even the evergreens have lightened up, with the lime shades of new growth fronting their somber wintergreen. And best of all, the blackflies have begun to go out of season.

So in this transition weekend between months, what is there to complain about? For now, we have the state pretty much to ourselves. The skiers and the college kids have gone away, and the summer people haven't arrived yet.

You can drive the interstates and from one mile marker to another you can count the oncoming cars without running out of fingers, in this moment of quiet when the tulip petals are falling down and the irises are budding up and the Indian paintbrushes freckle lawns with orange dots.

But it won't last, this time when Vermont is our own. *They* are coming. They always do, and the vanguard is already in motion. They drive cars with license plates reading Ohio and New Jersey and Virginia, and they think Vermont is a neat place, in the summertime.

49

And right behind them comes the main invasion. Well, the Florida invasion. There is a snowbird inversion in Florida at the end of May. Some awesome force turns the state upside down, and people's ancestors come spilling out onto the highways, heading north. Some of them steer by looking under the top of their steering wheels, and they all drive too slow in huge cars that make them feel safe.

Add to them the hordes of southbound Canadians who all drive too fast, and you get a volatile mix on the highways, a risk level that drives prudent Vermonters to the back roads, which are prettier anyway.

The visitors come here to find an America they can't touch any more at home. One where fields and forests and villages still form a pattern that delights the eye, especially when you throw in pastures speckled with black and white cows waiting to have their pictures taken by people from Away. Those cows are the secret to the Vermont landscape, but the visitors don't think of them as economic engines.

Somehow though, the summer people learn the mythology that when those cows lie down, it's going to rain.

That's a harmless illusion, probably started by a gossipy farmer whose cows did indeed lie down before some storm. There are talkative farmers in Vermont. There must be. But Vermont cows are no more predictive of the weather than is that rodent from Pennsylvania who is trusted to tell us how long the winter will be.

Cows are just as likely to go to the barn before it rains, or to cluster in one corner of their pasture before it rains, or simply to do what they usually do: stand around trying hard to chew cud and look smart at the same time.

Our impressionable visitors seek out the country

roads, overcoming their fear of getting told "You can't get there from here," in the pleasure of experiencing the Vermont difference. And in the process, of course, they clutter up the state.

All that is a nuisance, but hardly enough to complain about. That's because summer hardly lasts long enough to become a fixture in the mind. When winter is one season out of four and yet takes up half the year, there's not much time for the other three seasons to catch our attention.

So pretty soon the summer people will go away, and the students will come back, and the leaf peepers will clog up the more scenic back roads, and then the skiers will be back. So what is there to complain about? After all, each surge of flatlanders is like the flooding of the Nile, adding another layer of richness to the land it covers.

No complaints about that.

But I'd love to nail down one fact. If old people drive twenty miles an hour too slow, and Canadians drive twenty miles an hour too fast, then how fast do old Canadians drive?

New England's Mississippi

The exact border between New Hampshire and Vermont is not etched in stone. It's fluid, you might say, and it changes a little every year.

The boundary is the Connecticut River, the biggest stream in New England. It has had a huge role in the settling of Vermont, and to a lesser extent, New Hampshire.

The exact boundary line was already in dispute back when people west of the river decided to split off and become Vermont, and decided that New Hampshire should be kept to the east, on the other side. New Hampshire was the older, stronger political unit, and so New Hampshire dictated the exact boundary line.

The river, they said, is in New Hampshire. All of it. And that view prevailed on appeal.

So now, whatever is wet is theirs and whatever stays dry is ours. And because the spring high water changes the riverbanks from time to time, dissolving mudflats here and piling them up there, so changes the border.

None of that matters to the paddlers and floaters and power-boaters who have reclaimed the waterway now that the high water of spring has receded again.

Many of the boaters who carve wakes on the Connecticut these days are just larking about, out to see what lies around the bend of the river.

52 They are unconsciously echoing other boaters, who worked their way up and down the stream centuries ago,

exploring and exploiting. The Connecticut was the first Interstate highway in northern New England.

As such, it played as significant a role for us as that bigger river did farther west.

If Mark Twain had lived in Hanover instead of Hannibal, would *Huckleberry Finn* still have been an American literary classic? Does the book depend on its geography, or would New England's Mississippi have done just as well? Suppose Huck and Jim had floated down the Connecticut River?

Ridiculous, you say, on the Connecticut there was no slavery overlay to add texture to the story.

Well, let's keep this in perspective, in scale. The Mississippi bisects America. The Connecticut bisects New England. In both cases the rivers rise in boggy lakes near the Canadian border, and each empties into an arm of the Atlantic far to the south.

Okay, so the Connecticut is only four hundred miles long, and the Mississippi flows for 2400 miles. Okay, so the biggest river in New England drains parts of four states, and the Mississippi and its tributaries reach into thirty states. And several of those tributaries are far larger than the Connecticut.

And then there's the legend thing. The *Natchez* and the *Robert E. Lee* don't stage riverboat races on the Connecticut. *Old Man River* is not sung about our river. And the Connecticut just sort of trickles into Long Island Sound at a place called Old Saybrook, without ever passing a community as vibrant or as tragic as New Orleans.

But in its place, and in proportion, the Connecticut is a mighty stream. It divides and unites four of the six northeastern states.

And like the Mississippi, it's been busy for a long time.

The Connecticut was the waterway that allowed explorers and settlers to penetrate the densely forested interior of upper New England.

Most of them came from Rhode Island in colonial times, and settled where the river would let them, in Brattleboro and Hanover and Wells River and White River Junction.

Soon the river was floating timber from the great northern forest out to market. And then its moving waters provided industrial power, and jobs for new immigrants from Quebec and for refugees from famine in Ireland. Later it provided electricity and still does. But now, it's back as it began, cleaner than it's been in a century and once again a pathway for canoes.

But more than all that, the river keeps Vermont and New Hampshire apart, to the evident satisfaction of people on both banks.

They're headstrong over there, literally. They won't pass a helmet law for motorcycles because they think it infringes on their right to, as their license plate says, "Live Free or Die." Without those helmets, they do both.

Agriculture thrives better in Vermont than in New Hampshire. Their north is way under-populated, their south is an annex of Massachacho and their leading newspaper has the subtlety of a cudgel.

We, on the other hand, are an oasis of culture and light, and they think we're way too liberal.

It's a good thing that river is there, even if they claim the entire stream. Of course the good part of that is, they have to pay for building and fixing up all the bridges that cross it. After all, they are in New Hampshire.

New England's Mississippi. It fits us. Now all we need is a hot novelist like Mark Twain to make our river legendary too. Do you suppose Chris Bohjalian could take on that task in his next novel? Or maybe Joe Citro, who writes horror stories, could do something with a merger plot.

No, that would be too horrible to contemplate.

Launching Season

Over the next week or so, launching season comes to Vermont. Thousands of new vessels will slide into troubled waters, as their designers watch anxiously to see whether they are seaworthy.

I'm the co-designer of two ships constructed in the boatyard called Milton High School, but those vessels sailed away years ago.

This year's class is being launched from high schools all over the state. It will be done in my town and in all the others with as much dignity and ceremony as the participants can stand, in the new summer heat.

I was taken to a real ship launching once, at the old Brooklyn Navy Yard. I was about five, and a new cruiser was joining the fleet during World War Two. There was a band, and people made speeches from a crude stand draped in bunting. A lady swung a bottle on a rope against the grey wall of the bow. She had to do it twice before the bottle broke, to loud cheers.

I remember men with sledgehammers knocking away some wedges underneath, and the ship began to slide backward, entering the water stern first with a great splash. I thought it would turn and sail off immediately to go help my father in the Pacific, but it was tethered to a dock instead. I was told the ship's innards were still unfinished, and it was not yet ready to function.

56

That's not true of this year's crop of high school graduates.

Up on the stage erected in the gym there's a knot of

people we have elected or appointed to supervise the building of new adults. They will hand out certificates to the graduates, attesting that their innards are now finished, by high school standards, and that they're officially ready to function independently.

The documents will say the graduates have absorbed an acceptable proportion of the English and math and history, and all the other stuff they've had poured into them for the past twelve years. The diplomas serve notice on employers and admissions officers that here's another batch of finished products out of the great American assembly line of education.

Some of them are glowing, and bedecked with the symbols of success in high school. There are the white sashes of the National Honor Society scattered through the crowd, and the gold cords that signify academic excellence.

Others look stoic. They have endured twelve years of being told where to go and what to do, and they will put up with this last bit of ado, even though they'd rather not. They're not going to college or to the armed services. They are about to realize the only goal they've ever had: to get out of high school.

Not one of them realizes that the cherished roll of paper with the word "diploma" on it is also an eviction notice. When they walk out of the gym and into the bright sunshine wearing those caps and gowns, with the cord carefully shifted to the other side of the mortar-board cap, they can't go back.

One minute they're seniors, masters of the high school world, and the next minute they're outsiders, moving uneasily into the ranks of alumni, suddenly part of their school's past. Oh, they'll be back for the next homecoming game, and there will be grins and hugs and all that, but there are new seniors now, and the high school world closes in on itself as it always does, and last year's grad is no longer an insider.

As they move from one world to the other, are the graduates ready for the transition? It's hard to tell if a vessel is shipshape by looking at its hull.

You can't inspect the innards of a ship, its plumbing and its wiring and its electronics, from the outside. And from the outside, you can't measure the life skills the graduate has acquired, the navigational tools that enable smooth sailing and the avoidance of rocks and shoals.

Is the graduate now armed with the qualities needed to weather the unfairness and injustice and adversity that exist beyond the high school walls? There's no report card that measures that part in the making of an adult, so all parents watch these ceremonies with mixed pride and apprehension, asking ourselves some tough questions.

What sort of vessel is being launched today? Have the values we've tried to instill taken hold? Were we firm enough when he was five, tolerant enough when she was ten?

For the most part, the shaping and forging and polishing are done now. The newly minted adult is in part what she has made of herself, what he has done with the raw materials we've tried to weld onto his emerging persona. Tolerance, generosity, integrity, selflessness, tenacity and patience. These things we have struggled to convey. Have we done enough? Will she be all right?

The new ship is underway under its own power, toward a destination of its own choice. Is it on course? Have we done enough? Is the Captain competent?

Something new to worry about. Something to replace, "Will she graduate?" Fresh concerns while the echo of a singular achievement still lingers.

JULY

"I'm the Best! Just Ask the Rest."

I am a modest little month, the lucky number seven.
But envied, don't you know, by all the other eleven.
You know that I'm the only one with no school days at all.
I am a modest little month, but I'm the best of all.

My sister June is so absorbed by cap and gown and bridal veil.
August is such a snob, he'd like to be called Au-GUST.
About the Brrs, Sep and Oct, and Nov and Dec, enough said.
Forget about the cold ones too, all the way through March.

April's such a sissy, she's crying all the time. And May?
Being green's not easy for Kermit, but May does it gracefully.
And then there's me. Modest little barefoot carefree me.
I'm the best. Come, play with me! Get high on July!

The Acrid Odor of Independence

Last night a kid touched off a firecracker near me, and I jumped. The kid wasn't trying to scare me. It's just that he had owned that firecracker for as long as he could stand it. After you imagine lighting it often enough, you have to light it.

I was about to say something harsh to that boy, when the smell got to me, the acrid odor of Independence Day.

On this Fourth of July there will be parades, of course. The local paper will have a float, and the Historical Society will too, and Henry Lamoreau will put all twelve of his black wreckers in line, and will drive the biggest. The Vietnam vets will march, and will try not to limp too much. The War Two vets will ride, and try not to notice that three of those who rode last year missed muster this time.

There will be band music, only a little oratory, and red-white-and-blue decorations on the stores and homes. Yesterday the Fire Department put out the flags on their telephone pole brackets along River Street and the rest of the parade route. And tonight, fireworks in the park.

There will be, in short, a feast for the eye and the ear, but it's the nose that triggers memories, dredges up images of Independence Days long gone.

The powder smell from one firecracker can startle the mind into opening old doors.

There's one just opening now. Let's go through.

Okay, on this side it's July 4th, 1949. See that kid over

there in the driveway? That's Billy Weygandt. He's three years older than we are, and he knows a lot of stuff. We're not supposed to hang around Billy Weygandt. Mom says he's a lot like Huckleberry Finn, more appealing to kids than to adults.

There's a lot of firecracker smoke in the air. Little kids have little firecrackers called ladyfingers, and we bigger kids have bigger firecrackers. They come in paper packages with pictures of Chinese dragons on them, and they're always red. The fuses are braided at the end of the package, and you have to be careful not to pull them loose while you're separating the firecrackers.

Remember the year Billy Weygandt had cherry bombs? He could launch a dogfood can about fifty feet straight up with a cherry bomb. Of course one didn't go off until he stuck his finger under the can to see what was wrong. Bang, and he was yelling and spraying blood all over the place, and they took him off to the hospital.

What made an old-fashioned Fourth old-fashioned was unfettered access to fireworks. That ended the year Billy Weygandt blew the end off his finger. The next year he wasn't much interested in launching dogfood cans to the treetops, and the storekeepers didn't seem to have much in the way of firecrackers. Hey kid, want some sparklers?

Look, there's another old door opening. That's the twins, Jimmy and Jerry, and their cousin OtherJimmy, wrapping crêpe paper around the spokes of their bikes for the annual patriotic bike contest up at the school this afternoon. They can take a lot of decorating, those old Schwinns. Jimmy and Jerry always finish in a tie for second place behind some kid whose parents do all the decorating. OtherJimmy never wins anything. Not fair.

You know, lately I haven't heard any stories about

kids blowing off the ends of their fingers with firecrackers. Guess it isn't really an old-fashioned Fourth after all. Maybe next year we can decorate the bikes with crêpe paper.

The Fourth of July could just as easily have been the Second, you know. On the second the Continental Congress agreed on a resolution to declare Independence, and they didn't all sign it until some time in August. What they did on the Fourth was to review Thomas Jefferson's text, and approve it, with some edits.

So when in the course of human events it came time to select one day as Independence Day, the Fourth it was. Fitting too, so George M. Cohan the Yankee Doodle Dandy could boast of being born on The Day. So was Calvin Coolidge, in Plymouth, Vermont, but being Calvin Coolidge, he didn't make a career out of bragging about it.

The significance of the Fourth was not cemented into the consciousness of the young nation until half a century later when the words of the dying John Adams were widely quoted.

He said, "At least Jefferson lives," and expired, not knowing that Thomas Jefferson had died a few hours earlier in Monticello on that same Fourth of July in 1826.

Fireworks have almost always been part of the celebration. So much a part of the day that using fireworks for other purposes, like celebrating a home run at the ballpark, seems vaguely sacrilegious.

The smell. The afterburn residue of the silver-gray powder every kid has discovered inside a firecracker. Fitting that it should be such a powerful stimulant to the memory.

In the smell of gunpowder, the United States was born, and in the smell of gunpowder, whether the black grains of early America or the cordite of modern weapons, the United States has been sustained. The odors are first cousins to those of the playtime explosions we use to mark anniversaries of the day we decided to become a nation, and to fire shots in anger to win our independence, and to keep it.

The nose knows.

It conjures up a Fourth of July evening of still air when young people, more or less supervised, fire whistling rockets and shrieking screamers out over Lake Champlain. The most impressive of them remind you of the Big Bang theory of how the Universe got started, and look for an instant like dandelion seeds about to take wing.

See over there? A kid is dancing barefoot on the grass with a spitting sparkler in each hand, as the dusk goes down through gray to deep blue on its way to night. He is twirling, giddy, that barefoot kid, carving great arcs in the air with his glowing wands. In a few minutes he'll collapse onto grass already gathering dew, as utterly spent as the rods in his hands.

I know that kid. He is me.

Wings above the Water

The pre-steam literature of the sea is full of phrases describing newly spotted distant vessels as "hull down," "over the horizon"; so far away that the ship itself cannot be seen, only the sails above it.

That is even possible on Lake Champlain, although it's only twelve miles wide. It's a hundred miles long and there are places where sky and water meet on the horizon with no intervening strip of land, and where distant boats cannot be seen. Sails appear as wings above the water, seemingly unfettered by any supporting structure.

In July, Lake Champlain comes alive with boats. Oh there are always some around from ice-out in the spring until after Thanksgiving. Most people on the water at the cold extremes of the boating season are addicts, obsessed by the intricacies of bass fishing. Their boats are simply another tool to get them to the battleground, to that mythical stretch of shoaling weedy water where they know the Big One lurks.

They pilot open outboards and they endure epic hardships for the chance to match wits with their prey. If they're lucky, they will keep one, to pan-fry or to bake. And they are oddly regretless about failure, about those days when they return fishless. They believe that a day spent fishing is not subtracted from their lifespans, whether they catch anything or not.

They know the lake intimately and over the decades they have found the spots where the bass are likely to be.

They will *not* tell you where those places are, nor will they take you there.

Most of the people who go afloat on the lake are much less intense about it, less picky about where they go, and much more picky about when they go. That's why July is such a big month for fair weather sailors. So many boats go into the water in the weeks surrounding July 4th that I'm sure the lake level rises an inch or so to compensate for all that hull displacement.

Most boats and most docks are pulled out of the lake not long after Labor Day, because moving ice does terrible things to them. They come back on trailers in July, some to rest on moorings, some to snuggle into marina slips and some to be drawn out again at day's end.

These boats are different from those used by the solo fishermen. They have cabins and some have toilets and bunks. They're bigger and faster and much more expensive. Sprinkled among them are the sailboats, whose masts wobble about like mobile lightning rods above the rows of neatly tied off powerboats in marinas. Most sailboats are immersed for the season, and ride on moorings in fair weather or foul.

They're the ones that draw the eye. The stately grace of their motion somehow endows the human soul with a dose of peace. And that's just the effect of watching them glide by.

The main lake, that is the part south and west of Grand Isle, is crowded with boats, a lot of them sailboats, in July and August. They come sweeping out of Mallet's Bay and the Burlington harbor and Shelburne Bay for day trips or weekend voyages on the waters where America's first naval battles were fought, back when Benedict Arnold was still an American hero.

But there's another part of Lake Champlain that's

almost a secret. It's called the Inland Sea, and it's the section north of the Route 2 causeway and east of Grand Isle, stretching up past St. Albans to Alburgh and beyond.

The Inland Sea is almost landlocked. The only way in and out for a big boat is through The Gut, the narrow passage between North Hero and South Hero Islands.

A lot of big boats just don't bother to sail the Inland Sea, and that's just fine, because it keeps clutter out of the view. There's nothing quite as restful as watching an occasional thirty foot sailboat drifting south toward Appletree Bay on a north wind.

When there's a south wind, the sailors cluster off the north end of Savage Island. The sandy bottom offers calm waters and a spot for lunch, a swim or an overnight.

Lake Champlain boaters, especially visiting French Canadian sail boaters, tend to be indifferent about clothing on board on the sunnier days in July and August. The boats are few, the distances are vast, and most Vermonters don't care and don't stare. In a state with a cherished tradition of skinny-dipping, what other people wear on the lake is pretty much their own business.

The basic difference between sail boaters and motor boaters is that the sailors are never in a hurry, and motor people always are.

To me, there's nothing relaxing about pounding along as fast as possible over choppy waves that whack the hull and the kidneys alike. On the other hand, wind is fickle and sailing requires constant alertness to the angles and force of the breeze.

My compromise is sometimes called a booze barge. On a pontoon boat you have the same sense of tranquility as on a sailboat, but there's less work. And cruising the lake at five or ten knots under the shade of an awning is far more restorative than whamming along at thirty or forty. I guess there's a boat for every purpose and every taste, and they're all in season on the lake in July and August.

And then there are "personal watercraft," those annoying things that sound like angry banshees and go howling around the lake leaving unburned gasoline in the water, a stench in the air, and an assault on the ear.

I go to the lakeside to recharge my batteries. I go afloat on the lake for the same reason, to relax and to shed the stresses of the rest of my life.

Howling machinery doesn't allow that. Personal watercraft are expressions of selfishness and inconsiderate aggression against my peace.

I have a solution to the problem.

If I ever run for the Legislature again my campaign will be based on this promise:

I will introduce a bill to establish a season on personal watercraft, from Memorial Day to the Ides of October. An open season. Any weapon, any range, no bag limit, no penalty for collateral damage, and a small bounty, just for keeping score.

Green is a Summertime Thing

When pictures of the Earth are relayed from outer space they show a blue and white ball reflecting sea and clouds, and perhaps a bit of beige to indicate land. There's no green.

Green is the color of life on Earth, and it's too bad it doesn't travel well. Green fades with distance. Even on the clearest, sharpest days of summer, our famous Green Mountains go a little gray and blue in the far distance.

In the South, where the air is hazier and more humid, there are perfectly green mountains as well. But they were named from a distance. One range is called the Blue Ridge, and another is the Great Smokies, all because green is not a long-distance color.

Too bad about green. The Irish, who know quite a lot about green, say there are forty shades of it in their Emerald Island, where it never fades. But in most temperate climates, green fades with time as well as with distance. And in occasionally intemperate climates like ours, green is a sometime thing, a summertime thing. In Vermont, in northern Vermont in particular, the signs of that impermanence are already creeping in.

Here we are in July, the very centerpiece month of the summer, the time when we've had warm breezes and sunshine long enough to get used to them, and when summer still seems to stretch out endlessly ahead.

68

But look. What's that curly brown thing on the grass? It's a leaf. A dead leaf. They are sneaking into place. You never see the dead leaves of July falling off a tree like the bright wind-blown maple-leaf squalls of October.

They just appear. They never stand up and shout, "Look at me!" like the fall foliage does. They're just suddenly there, sere and withered, scutting along in a light breeze.

They are harbingers, the Cassandras of the northern woods, making predictions of things that will come true, whether we welcome that truth or not. These leaves are unwelcome, because they say, "Enjoy it while you can, we too, used to be green."

Probably they are birch leaves. Birches are notoriously undisciplined, and if any tree's leaves are going to remind us that summer is limited and green is not forever, Central Casting will assign the birches.

Robert Frost, the poet claimed in part by Vermont even though he was from Away, wrote kindly of birches, but they are the hooligans of the northern forest. You probably knew a kid in the seventh grade who was a lot like birches: wouldn't stand up straight, wore flashy clothes, a bit of a showoff . . .

You can tell when a storm approaches by the smell of the wind and the look of the clouds, and the scurry of people rushing to close windows and rescue dry laundry from the clothesline.

You can tell when the season of cold begins its approach, by the birch leaves that appear furtively on the ground. It's a sign to take seriously.

These few stray leaves may mean only that the tree they fell from is not healthy, but those same trees leaf out year after year, and endure. I prefer to think they're a sure sign that the air is soon to cool, the days soon to shorten.

It means the southbound geese will be heard and then

seen overhead, and the mountains will light up with the colors of fall, and then it will snow again.

Except for the evergreens which wear the somber side of green as if it were the color of a monastic habit, the color of life will soon be gone, and in northern Vermont, it won't be back until May.

At this moment in the high summer, when the color of spring shows its first sign of fading, it is cherished even more than when it is being newly minted in May. And this moment, the first hint of green's mortality, is the moment when you see that first furtive birch leaf.

So while you can, wink at something green.

". . . *And the Livin' is Easy*"

For most of the year living in Vermont requires exercise. It's like swimming upstream in a river; you have to expend energy just to stay even.

That rule is relaxed for a little while in the weeks after Independence Day.

The first hay crop is in, the second is too short to cut, and life slows down along the shoreline of Lake Champlain. The water is warm enough to swim in, more or less, and so people do, mostly people from Away, who come to Vermont because they can't find anything like it in Ohio or Virginia, or whatever down-country state their license plates proclaim.

The summer people form one of our annual migrations. Many of them have been summering here for decades, even for generations, but there are always enough new ones so that Vermonters get stopped occasionally by Flatlanders seeking directions.

That happens more frequently in towns where the Selectboard decides not to put up road signs. The locals already know the road names, and where those roads lead. Why spend taxpayers' money to provide a convenience that would only benefit someone from Away?

What a wonderfully dismissive term that is. "He's from Away." It's used as an implicit excuse for whatever Flatlander behavior has drawn your attention. It also conveys a complete indifference to the notion that Away is divided into parts that have names and identifiable traits. No matter, it's not Vermont.

Every true Vermonter, whether an RV or a Recover-

71

ing Flatlander, harbors a secret wish that he'll encounter summer people so thoroughly lost that the Vermonter can utter in all truth the classic line: "You can't get there from here."

Or if you're really lucky, one of them will ask, "Have you lived here all your life?" And you can say, "Not yet."

Those are the kinds of things that endear Vermont to the skiers and the leaf peepers, all our seasonal visitors who come here for the Vermont difference.

There is an internal conflict in Vermont over how to preserve the echoes of an older, simpler America that visitors think they find in quaint villages, sweeping vistas and green pastures sprinkled with black and white cattle, all very photogenic.

Is that all there is? Is Vermont destined to be a huge theme park for the America evoked by Robert Frost and Norman Rockwell? Are we an outdoor museum celebrating a Currier-and-Ives countryside?

And if so, is that a viable future, or even a respectable one? The questions about what kind of Vermont we should be trying to build got shocked onto the front burner a few years ago.

The National Trust for Historic Preservation put the entire state of Vermont on its list of endangered places in 1993, sharpening the debate over whether we want to retain and develop tourism as our chief industry.

To do that, if we want to, we must first secure the future of the dairy farms that underpin all the photogenic features of the landscape. They make possible the working landscapes that surround the tidy villages, and they are endangered because the price of milk is beyond the control of the families that produce it and is too often too low to cover the costs of milking.

There are voices here saying that Vermont has to

move beyond picturesque and quaint, that a vibrant economy depends more on IBM than on maple syrup, that manufacturing trumps bed-and-breakfast in the Vermont economy.

We've been having that debate for years, and it will ebb and flow into the future. In the meantime, people are still drawn here for the Vermont difference, however they may define it. The summer people provide a bit of lift for our economy, and a bit of a chuckle. They're part of the panorama of our seasons.

The summer people are followed by the ones who come in September and October to gape at dead maple leaves, and then by those who come to fall downhill on expensive sticks in the winter.

Besides, the summer people know something that the more hurried visitors in other seasons miss: the simple pleasure of watching an old moon etch a silver highway across the surface of a lake. All you have to know is how to sit still.

And now, when the living is as easy as it ever gets here, Vermont is very good at teaching people from Away how to sit still.

AUGUST

The Night Lights of August

The sun reddens and the hills exhale across untroubled waters,
shivering the surface into ripples that drift away, becoming waves.
That offshore breeze enables a beach-fire lighting of the night.
A kitchen match helps old gray driftwood grow new orange twigs
whose light dances on sun-touched faces and bottoms-up boats.

Hovering marshmallows do an anti-bleach
in the glow of a golden quilt of coals.
In an ecstasy of ignition sparks leap toward the stars.
How bold! How futile.

Where there's light there must be heat. Tonight it's mating heat,
as fireflies flash and rise, sifting the night for Mister Goodlight.

The darkness deepens, framing other lights.
White—Lamp away on an island where the wires never went.
Yellow—Headlights strobing out between the trunks of distant trees.
Green—One last boat across the lake, running for the ramp.
Gold—Another beach fire, too far off to flicker.

Night matures a little more and points of light appear.
You can find the farther shore; just connect the dots.

The Front-Row Seats Get Wet

In theaters, arenas and ballparks, the closer you are to the action, the plushier the seating gets.

My arena is Lake Champlain, with the Adirondacks forming a dramatic backdrop, and in the evening the menacing lights of the state prison at Dannemora glow from a hillside up beyond Plattsburgh, over in New York.

My seat is in the front row, but it's not fancy. It's just canvas on a metal frame, and it conforms readily to a pear-shaped body. I sit where grass slopes away to the wave-rounded flat shale stones that make this beach stone-skipping heaven on quiet days. There's another chair over by the cottonwood; bring it over.

The wavelets slap vigorously against the shoreline when the wind is from the south, and pat the beach calmly on the north wind, when we're in the lee of a nearby point. We even build up a little sand here when that happens.

That wave-lapping goes on at the front of the stage. Just beyond, kids and grandkids float and shriek and dive like little ducks. Out farther, beyond the raft, the water skiers and wake boarders cut their curves across the surface, and if they're thoughtful, try to stay away from the trolling fishermen in the deep trench between here and the centerline of the Inland Sea, Cedar and Fishbladder and Savage Islands. They don't know that Mr. Bigbass lives under the raft, and I'm not telling. Besides they're after lake trout and landlocked salmon.

Farther out yet, the sailboats work the wind. Today

76

it's blowing down from Canada, bringing a slightly cooler touch to the face.

That will change though. Way over there behind Dannemora Prison the biggest show of all is building up. The anvil of the sky is rising in the northwest as a thunderhead rockets up forty thousand feet and spreads out, white and flat at the top. But it's what's going on at the bottom that bears watching. It's time to secure the boat covers.

Isn't it odd that every change in the clouds, every loss of sunlight, triggers a response. You don't want to run around yelling "batten down the hatches," but there are prudent things to do.

Only in August do these mighty storms come roaring out of the Adirondacks and sweep across the lake into Vermont, bringing an inch or two of rain and gusts of wind that can take out a tree.

Oh, it rains at other times, and quite a lot. But August is for the big boomers.

See over there? Yes, beyond Savage Island. The ridge above Dannemora is dimming, obscured by the oncoming rain.

Excuse me a minute, I'm going to check the car windows.

See the lightning? Lots of it today, and the wind has dropped to nothing. Look at the cottonwood leaves. They seem frozen, and they'll wiggle in the slightest wind. Feel how still the air is, don't you think it's a bit oppressive? People say you can smell rain in the air, but my nose isn't very good. I think you can feel it coming though. It's not exactly a tingle, just a sense that something powerful is pending, and the eye measures its approach.

One of the gems of American music is Ferde Grofé's *Grand Canyon Suite*, with its vivid movement on the passing of a cloudburst through the most majestic landscape of the Southwest. I wonder what a gifted composer could do with the drama now sweeping onto the west coast of New England.

See the feathers on the water, the little ruffles? Here comes the wind.

I'll be right back. I want to see if there's laundry on the line.

There. One, two, three, four, thunder. All right, it's about five miles away, but it's coming.

I thought it might go around us to the north and whack St. Albans, but it doesn't look like that's going to happen. St. Albans catches more than its share of summer thunder, but I guess not today. See, Grand Isle is gone, and that gray haze is the rain. You'll see the nearer islands blank out too, soon enough.

See that line of little clouds scudding along in front of the rest? That's the four-minute warning, more or less. Oh sure, everything is orchestrated in these storms. It all unfolds according to the script, but it never, ever gets boring.

Look at that moron out there in his little boat, running into the weather. Why doesn't he duck behind an island? He's gonna get caught out in it.

There goes Fishbladder, another island lost behind the rain. In a moment you'll see a dark line on the water, way out. That's where the hard rain is hammering the surface.

I love sitting on this little chair until the last moment, because the more the storm builds up, the smaller I feel. Don't you think it's proper to feel really small when Nature is flexing its muscles?

Okay, there goes Savage Island, and that's the end of sitting out. Leave the chairs. We've got about enough time to get onto the porch and move some stuff away from the rain.

Here comes that dark line, with a few big rainsplats ahead of it.

What? Can't hear you, the rain's too loud. Wow! How do you like the show? That was close. You can almost smell the ozone.

Look at the drops bounce off the deck and dance on the glass-top table. You could drown a frog in this rain! And talk about dancing, look at the trees! These old cottonwoods are pretty tough when they're healthy. This one's been standing here on the beach for almost a hundred years, taking whatever the wind can do.

But back inland there's a stretch along the road to Milton where every couple of years a wind like this will whip through and knock down trees, and it's always within the same half-mile. One of my neighbors always puts his chain saw in his truck after a storm like this, just in case he's the first one along the road after a knockdown.

Whew! Good thing this kind of rain doesn't last very long. It seems to be letting up a little already. And look over there to the west. There's a patch of sunshine moving across the prison. It'll be here in about twenty minutes, and the air will be cooler. And by sunset, those canvas chairs ought to be dry enough to sit in again.

Have I told you about the sunsets here? Ah, just wait.

The Hell You Say It Ain't So

The air is so still there's not one wiggling leaf on the cottonwood tree that hangs over the lake. And it's hot. Muggy, drippy, steamy hot.

Shade is supposed to relieve the assault of sunlight, and it does, but that doesn't mean it's cooler there.

Even the lake is hot. There's something obscene about lukewarm lake water. The temperature has leached all the refreshing quality out of the water, and the heat breeds the kind of algae blooms that signify that Lake Champlain's health is fragile. This is the same lake that wears an ice cap two feet thick on the other side of the year, in February.

Back then it was so cold we only imagined this kind of heat. Oops! We got what we wished for, and we're out of wishes.

It's hotter than Hell. Somehow it helps to say that, although the expression is now as endangered as the black-footed ferret.

A group of theologians in the Church of England has stated that Hell is not as bad as it has been pictured in generations of scary sermons by fire-and-brimstone preachers.

No molten pit, say the new thinkers, no eternal fire. Not even the traditional weeping and gnashing of teeth associated with being there.

Of course there is a price for all that theorizing. It has caused other theologians to consign the revisionists to the very Hell they don't believe in any more for heresy.

But the implications of that declaration are widespread, and for the English language, appalling.

Some of our most graphic and cherished expressions are suddenly obsolete. Bats like the dark and flee the light. Something moving very fast, they say, is going like a bat out of Hell. But if Hell isn't as bright as we thought, the bats need not flee.

If Hell has been rehabilitated, then, when everything goes wrong at once, we can't say all Hell broke loose. And a large number of our literary heroes may now be asked to rewrite some of their best lines. Must John Milton now revisit Paradise Lost to remove the line, *Better to reign in Hell than to serve in Heaven?*

What about gentle Emily Dickinson's lament that parting is all we know of Heaven and all we need of Hell? Doesn't a non-threatening Hell take some of the zing out of such sweet sorrow? The poet Shelley said Hell is a city much like London, a populous and smoky city. But if there's no fire, how can there be smoke? Fog yes, but other poets and the makers of raincoats have pre-empted London's version of fog.

And what about Dante's inferno? Won't the seventh circle of Hell have to be redesigned now?

August days can no longer be hotter than Hell, and we can't tell each other on those hot days, to go there.

And who's going to rescue the central casting old-timers in the western movies? The ones who stand around on the edges of the crowd while somebody else talks about how much trouble the hero is in. And then this old guy spits, and plucks on his one suspender, and says, *Why, he ain't got the chance of a snowball in Hayull.*

If Hell hath no fury, then the wrath of a woman scorned is not such a dreadful force. But we all know better. Well, some of us do.

AUGUST

Too bad about all those expressions.

Hell's Bells, we'll have to replace them with images equally forceful and graphic, and it may take us until Hell freezes over to do it. But it's too hot to think about that now.

Reunion Season

The calendar says it's August, and that's true, but not descriptive enough, not precise. This is really reunion season.

Clumps of related people from all over the country try to make up for living apart by getting together once in a while, to repair and renew the ties that connect them, the fabric of family.

In mine they arrive from eight states, northwest and midwest and southeast and northeast.

The roster is subject to change, of course. Long-absent old-timers become the stars of campfire legends. A dog dead four decades is still famous for trying to retrieve a mooring buoy from the lake, and almost drowning in the effort. There are two new babies since the last reunion three years ago, both up and running, and very mobile, to say nothing of loud.

And there's a new second wife, who's sort of on trial. You see, everyone liked WifeOne, so WifeTwo's acceptance depends to some degree on the impression she makes on a tough jury, the outlaws.

Those who marry in are called outlaws to distinguish them from their parents, the in-laws. The wives of two of the brothers will make the call for the rest of the family. Nobody elected them; the family dynamic just works that way. The outlaws will watch the two children that WifeTwo has brought into the clan, to see whether they've been raised, or merely fed.

A reunion is a chance for young cousins to learn that

83

their nuclear families are part of a larger molecule, scattered as it may be.

"You hillbillies talk funny," says one set of cousins on the first day.

"Don't you call me a hillbilly, you carpetbaggin' Yankee!"

The War Between the States has been over for almost 150 years, and it ended before most of the cousins' ancestors arrived in America. But honor must be satisfied, and so two nine-year-olds have a minute of brisk exercise, in which each discovers that the other is also a red-blooded American, and then they go swimming together.

Teen cousins discover that the boys have gotten really tall in the past three years, and that the girls have a suddenly elegant architecture. Those discoveries will cost them the play-pal relationship of past reunions, and spark an interest in when kinship becomes thin enough to allow them to be kissing cousins. Most of the mothers would vote, "Never!"

The sing-along doesn't work. The boomers who lead it are miffed that the new generation can't walk their bridge over troubled waters, and don't know the lyrics to *Hey Jude* and *Michelle*. The boomers insist that nothing written since their time *has* any lyrics worth knowing. The sixty-somethings look smug and remind each other that their parents said the same thing about Jerry Lee Lewis and Little Richard.

So they try a compromise, something they think everybody should know.

You've got to know when to hold 'em, know when to fold 'em,

Know when to walk away, and know when to run.
That's no better.

"It doesn't, like, speak to me," says a teen-something

whose mother is silently condemned by the outlaws for "allowing" her to wear a nose ring.

And if achieving harmony is difficult among the humans, it's worse among the dogs. Most of them are big dumb happy ball-chasers who slobber and shake water all over everybody.

But one of the daughters-in-law insists on bringing a snarly little beast who's despised by most of the people, and by the host pooch. He does not permit poaching out of his food bowl, and tries to teach the critter some manners.

"Get that cannibal off my dog!" Now it's tongue-biting time as well as dog-biting time. Time *not* to say, "If you had a dog instead of a fuzzy rat, this wouldn't be happening."

For a day or so the tensions among these intergenerational, intercultural branches of the family tree threaten to smother the bonding that being there is supposed to produce.

The kids don't care that they're all descended from an Irish couple who met in Maine after coming to America separately from adjacent parts of County Galway in the West of Ireland. Some of them don't even know what a leprechaun is.

And things get noticed, negative things. Has Uncle Ralphie always been as self-centered as he seems now? Did you hear how that kid talks to his mother?

And then the child who threw a tantrum because Uncle Steve would not allow a beach fire when the wind blew toward the house, makes a breakthrough and does the rite-of-passage swim out to the raft. A five-year-old catches a fish. All right, a six-inch perch, but still a real first fish, and she's not required to clean it.

A ten-year-old gets to run the outboard motor and a

nine-year-old learns to sail a Sunfish. One of the fifty-somethings has a warm chat with Miss Nose-Ring, and discovers a real person inside the persona.

One of the eighty-somethings teaches a campfire crowd to sing *Anne Boleyn*. And for three days kids go around with soccer balls under their arms, looking truculent and bellowing:

With 'er 'ead tucked underneath 'er arm, she walks the bloody Tower.

With 'er 'ead tucked underneath 'er arm, at the midnight hour.

And suddenly the magic works. The design is fulfilled. A kid looks at one of those stiff photos of the immigrant family and asks which one is my great-grandmother, and what was her name?

"Family" comes front and center. The cultural and generational walls melt and everybody from rug rat to grandma feels connected to something special. We are somebody. We have each other. I'm related to some nice people, and I want to see them again. That's what reunions are for.

And I've got three years to repair the sail, find the lost softballs and hope somebody else's dog snacks on the fuzzy rat before the next one.

Out of Season

"The early bird gets the worm." That bit of folk wisdom has been used for centuries to explain the obsessive behavior of robins. It celebrates earliness as a virtue. I suppose it's related to that other smug adage, the one you can blame on Ben Franklin: "Early to bed and early to rise, makes a man healthy, wealthy and wise."

In 1940 the humorist James Thurber turned that around. "Early to rise and early to bed makes a male healthy, wealthy and dead."

In earlier times earliness was not so exalted. Thousands of years ago there was more of a sense of proportion about the performing of obligations.

"To every thing there is a season, and a time for every purpose under Heaven."

That's better. The Book of Proverbs suggests that things ought to happen when they're due, and not before. Robins, take heed. There is indeed a time for things to happen, for the changes we expect as the year turns.

In Vermont that means new life rushes into the trees and bushes in early May. In November the skiers appear, and in April the geese come back. Each arrives in its season.

Toward the middle and end of September, the maples color up, drawing in Vermont's biggest seasonal migration, the leaf peepers. They come because the colors are uniquely spectacular around here, and that's a boon to the Vermont economy.

Leaf season starts about the middle of September,

87

and usually extends well into October. So what's going on this year?

For the record, this is summertime. Suntans, lemonade, bare feet and luxuriant greenery. It's important to establish that, because summertime is under assault.

You can see the evidence of that on Route 7, the Main Street of westerly Vermont.

Along Route 7 in the Champlain Valley there are a lot of mature maples that ought to know better, already dressed in their best leaf peeper colors, and it's only the third week in August. Unseemly, and unseasonal.

Plant physiologist John Shane of the University of Vermont has noticed the early coloring up. "We know a lot about the chemistry of fall foliage," he says. "But we don't know much about what triggers it."

Shane thinks the early showing may occur more often in roadside trees, and that some kind of stress may be involved: exposure to road salt in the winter, or too much water in the spring. But, he says, it's guesswork.

It's easier to figure out which trees to watch. They're the same sugar maples every year, and it's easy to be misled by their signals. No matter what those confused trees proclaim, it's still pre-season for leaves. The National Football League has yet to play a game that matters, the Red Sox are still alive, school hasn't started, and Labor Day is still ahead. All those things will happen in their season, but not yet.

You hear that, you leaves? Your time will come, and in just a few weeks. But there's no advantage to being the early bird among trees, in being the one in which the colors are early to rise. In fact it's a worrisome and not-so-welcome foretaste of short, darker days ahead.

If that harbinger of fall draws down the corners of your mouth here in August, take comfort in the Proverb. "To every thing there is a season."

Hey, you maples. It's not here yet.

SEPTEMBER

Pretender

September is a pretender,
entering as the annex of August.

But within a span of days
it clearly isn't summer any more.

The blue infinity of sky implodes
into streaks of ragged clouds.

Too full to fly, they fall across the hills,
impaled on spearpoints of spruce.

The trees pretend to summergreen
but bronze appears, and yellow too.

A few precocious maples
flare into Octoberglow

And yet the grass grows on,
pillowing the browning leaf that says,

"What falls in autumn withers."

Awaken hibernating sweaters and listen to the sky.
there's gossiping aloft as tribes of geese go by.

September.
Pretender.

Echo of August.
Foretaste of frost.

The Summer Kid Lingers

The little brother is still asleep when the summer kid gets up and creeps down the lakeside cottage's stairs. He has learned to step only near the wall, to keep the treads from squeaking.

Out through the kitchen (grab a cookie) and down the cliffside path to the rocky beach with Cinders, the black cocker spaniel.

He imagines that someone has shouted, "Go jump in the lake!" and so he does, staying away from the weed patch that tugs on his legs, and from the cold spot where the spring feeds in.

He has a round face and sunburn on his nose and the tops of his ears and there's no place on this Earth he'd rather be.

He's not quite a towhead anymore, and scalp shows through the short wet strands of an almost-white burr-cut.

He is eight-going-on-nine, and the going-on part is really important, because the nine part is only a few days off.

The summer kid is campaigning to be allowed to spend his birthday here at the lake, where he's learning to row and to fish, and to stay away from the splatty end of cows in a nearby barn.

It's not working, not negotiable. They'll have to go Away before the birthday, back to school in Virgina, back to Dad's job.

"But I could make up a few days of school."

"No."

"Why not?"

"Because Mom said," Mom said. The non-appealable Final Word. "And don't whine."

The last few days become extra precious. The summer kid makes a mental list.

Catch a bass.

Swim out to the raft, around it and back, non-stop.

Find the Three-Pine Trail, the legendary path to the ridge top, the one that Mom and Uncle Leonard climbed when they were summer kids.

Catch another frog.

Have a beach fire one night, with marshmallows.

Teach Cinders to retrieve sticks and balls from the water as well as he does from the grass.

Go visit the calf with the nubby horns and the Ohio-shaped patch of white on its black hide.

Beg a ride on the tractor, or at least on the ice-wagon behind it.

And if it rains, finish *Men of Iron,* the book about the kid who was training to be a knight.

Just the other day there was lots of time to do all those things, and now there's not.

The wife is still asleep when the summer kid gets up and creeps down the lakeside cottage's stairs. He built those stairs carefully, to keep the treads from squeaking.

Out through the kitchen (grab a cookie) and down the cliffside path to the rocky beach with Guinness, the golden retriever.

He imagines that someone has shouted, "Go jump in the lake!" and so he does, staying away from the weed patch that tugs on his legs, and from the cold spot where the spring feeds in.

He has a round face and sunburn on his nose and the tops of his ears, and there's no place on this Earth he'd rather be.

He's almost a towhead again, and scalp shows through the short wet strands of a white burr-cut.

He is sixty-five plus a few days, and those days make all the difference. He is retired now, and for the first time in his life, was able to spend his birthday here at the lake.

It's early September now, and he's got a list of things to do before the warm weather ends. It's already brisky at night, and the days are getting shorter.

Catch a bass.

Find the Three-Pine Trail.

Have a beach fire one night, with marshmallows.

Teach Guinness to retrieve balls and sticks from the grass as well as he does from the water.

Go skinny-dipping, now that the summer people are gone.

And if it rains, pull out that tattered old book about the kid who trained to be a knight.

A few days ago there was lots of time to do all those things, and now there's not.

No work, no need to move anywhere else now that the cottage is rebuilt and insulated, no real hurry.

Except that the seasons provide their own imperatives.

And soon the adult list will intrude.

Pull in the dock.

Paint the porch.

Winterize the boat.

Put away the yard furniture and the gas grill.

But not yet.

Although the adult list looms, the summer kid lingers, and does not yet have to become the adult.

Let's see, the Three-Pine trail is supposed to start near a cave where Uncle Bob once found raccoon bones. If he walks up through the old pasture . . .

Black and Orange Time

The colors of Halloween have been migrating forward in the calendar. There's already a big orange pumpkin on the front porch of a home in the village.

In combination black and orange are the colors of tigers. By themselves, black is for witches and their cats. Orange is for pumpkins and rising moons. All that is October stuff, when the windows of stores get decorated in seasonal themes, and when little fingers use dull scissors in grade-school classrooms to cut out silhouettes of black hats and broomsticks, or of jack o'lanterns.

And yet the colors of Halloween are here in September as well, in the erratic flight of Monarch butterflies and the unhurried crawl of wooly bear caterpillars.

To the casual eye the fluttering navigation of butterflies appears to have no purpose, unlike the other nectar-loving insects whose homeward dash we call a bee-line.

But the Monarchs do fly with a purpose, and quite soon now that purpose will be to go south and west for the winter, all the way to a remote mountain region in Mexico. There will probably be pictures published later this year of trees almost completely cloaked in the orange and black wings of Monarchs.

Now, they're stoking up on milkweed for the marathon flight, the way runners load up on carbohydrates the night before a long race.

Unfortunately the bright fluttering creatures favor our roads as temporary landing pads, and they're not quite agile enough to evade fast-moving cars. We will unintentionally collect quite a few of them on grilles and windshields.

We'll also account for quite a few wooly bear caterpillars, who have a tendency to ripple their way along where tires abound. Scientists say the width of the wooly bear's dark central stripe has no bearing whatsoever on how cold the winter will be.

Children and grandparents know better, and so do the readers of almanacs. Forecasting winter by the wooly bear's stripes in September is every bit as reliable as forecasting spring by the actions of a Pennsylvania rodent in February.

Why is it that the butterflies and caterpillars are so much more noticeable now than they were last month or even last week? Is it because we've come to regard them as signposts, as indicators of change in the air?

They are, after all, another sign that summer is over, and that a most remarkable time is almost upon us. Soon it will be colder and darker, and hibernating rakes will be awakened to confine the fall of leaves. We'll get reacquainted with wood smoke and wool, and with pumpkin pie and frosty breath.

Mother Nature is a gifted scorekeeper. She's about to take away the warmth we've treasured during the all-too-brief summer, but she offsets that take-away by making the transition our most spectacular season, a time when we feel invigorated and energized.

All that is still ahead, of course. The Monarch and the wooly bear will be among the missing when the fullness of fall arrives. Perhaps we need such messengers to bring us tidings of change, and that's what these welcome black and orange transients do, in their uniforms of fall's final colors.

Fierce, Man!

Fierceness is the quality that intimidates, that inspires terror because the fierce one appears to be so menacing. Tigers, for example, have a lot of fierce. Puppies have hardly any, but they grow into it.

So do little boys, but they need coaching.

Thump, thump. Clap, clap.

Those are nine-year-old palms thumping thigh pads and clapping each other.

They are the Milton Broncos, and they are fierce, man. This is how they intimidate the other team before a game.

Thump, thump. Clap, clap.

The opposing players are supposed to hear that, and it is supposed to chill them. The idea is to get them to think, "Man, those Milton Broncos are fierce!"

Thigh pad slapping is Lesson One in learning football.

Little-kid football is about learning a lot of things. Like how to put on thigh pads, and shoulder pads. And why they are important.

Crunch . . . "Ow!"

How to handle getting yelled at by a three hundred pound man wearing a whistle and the shreds of a drill-instructor's mentality.

How to take direction. How to co-operate. What teamwork is, and why it works. And sportsmanship. All the qualities that after-dinner speakers love to extol at sports awards banquets at the end of the season.

But at the level where the Broncos play, all that stuff

really works. Later, in high school and beyond, it's too late, the need to win gets in the way too much. But for now, in Bronco-ball the kids learn all the good stuff about football, because they have so much football to learn.

The numbers of the holes between defensive linemen. How to interpret what the quarterback is saying. And the rules, invoked by that three hundred pound man. *You can't do that, that's holding. You can't tackle a guy who doesn't have the ball.*

So when they play somebody, fierce is important. It might even mask the absence of skill.

Thump, thump. Clap, clap.

Intimidation is critical. And the miniature cheerleaders understand that. They jump up and down and shriek, taunting the opposite sideline.

"We got Jimmy Wilson on our side." They chirp, as if that makes all the difference. "We got Jimmy on our side."

And the other team is supposed to think, did you hear that? It's over, man. They got Jimmy Wilson on their side. Jimmy Wilson! The cheerleaders make it sound as if every Bronco is already in the Hall of Fame.

And here comes Jimmy, trotting onto the field. A little under seventy pounds. A little over four feet tall. A little over four feet wide, it seems with those huge shoulder pads and a little pimple of a helmet pushing out the top.

All that on legs that look like toothpicks stuck into a mushroom.

"We got Jimmy Wilson on our side!" To the tune of *He's got the Whole World in His Hand.*

Now they're all out there, all those Broncos, all thumpin' and clappin'.

Fierce, Man!

97

Thump, thump. Clap, clap.

"We got Jimmy Wilson!" Wow, those guys must be tough!

Those are the Milton Broncos, man. They may still be learning to block and tackle, and to run the ball, but they got Jimmy Wilson, man, and they got thump down cold.

Thump, thump. Clap, clap.

So glory must surely be just ahead.

Flo and Bert Alert

Yesterday morning I was driving north along one of our most scenic byways, Route 100, when Flo and Bert pulled onto the road in front of me in their Ohio Winnebago. I know who they are because their names are spelled out on the back of their bus-like vehicle in fancy calligraphy.

Flo and Bert are in Vermont to see the leaves, and from the speed they were going yesterday, they've seen every one of them. They are Flatlanders, people from Away, from down-country. They've come here in droves this month to clog up our back roads and to gape at a sight they could have stayed home to see.

In the fall, all across this country, leaves color up and drop off the trees. But the clever people who live in this rumpled back corner of New England have got everybody convinced that the autumn leaves color up best in Vermont. Well, they do. It's one of two places in the Northern Hemisphere where the effects of climate, altitude and tree species produce a truly spectacular fall display. The other hotspot is in Siberia, which is beyond the reach of a Winnebago from Ohio.

Flo and Bert are a sub-species of Flatlander called Leaf-Peepers. Bless their hearts, they are subject to persuasion. If the grass is greener on the other side of the fence, then the leaves must be redder on the other side of the state line, in Vermont. The state spends quite a lot of money getting that message out, over a soundtrack of "Autumn Leaves," and it pays off.

The leaf peepers will leave almost as many dollars in

99

Vermont as the leaves the trees will drop during foliage season. Well that's a stretch, but serious people say the autumnal invasion brings in about five hundred million dollars in a good-to-average year.

Maybe the Vermont secret is that this is a state of vest-pocket vistas.

You can't see forever on a clear day because the views keep getting in the way. I can almost hear Flo and Bert trying to take it all in.

"Flo, look at those colors!"

"Yes, Bert. Let's stop at that quaint little shop and look for souvenirs."

Well, that's how Vermont does it. This whole leaf thing is a lure to get Flo and Bert into one of those little shops, or restaurants or bed-and-breakfast inns. Inside every one of those places is a display of Flatlander Feeding Frenzy stuff.

Tree juice, for starters. Vermont's other big victory in the subtle art of persuasion is maple syrup. We have made everyone believe that tree juice boiled in the shadow of the Green Mountains is the true nectar of the North, while the same stuff made anywhere else is barely fit for drowning pancakes.

Downcountry people who buy Vermont maple syrup are smarter than those who don't, of course, but even they have no idea how much toil and luck goes into the making of that half-gallon jug or tin, or how important "sugar" is to the state's psyche.

And then there's black-and-white stuff. Vermont's favorite cows, the ones that decorate pastures so Flatlanders can use up their film, come in designer colors of black and white, slathered over their hides in random patterns. Vermont has everyone believing that any souvenir doodad in the shops is quainter, and cuter, and most important, costlier, if painted in the black and white of Holstein cows.

But don't discount the lure of the leaf, it's honest bait. In Vermont on a crispy day you can watch the colors of flame run along a ridge-line, and there's no smoke, and no blackened ruin when the colors fade.

You can watch an autumn wind slide a patch of sunlight across a hillside, igniting the colors below. You can be there when the great golden orange disc slips its tether and goes skating giddy down the wind. You can cause ten thousand fallen leaves to rise and dance again in the wake of your moving car.

You can observe one of Nature's most benign wonders, and while you do, Vermont will feed you and shelter you and sell you souvenirs. Flo and Bert will go back to Ohio believing that they have witnessed magic, in a state that's truly a place apart.

Part of the apartness that we cherish and that visitors savor is the relationship we have with that big sturdy tree that provides us with furniture, floors and firewood, in addition to its other economic advantages.

Vermonters owe a lot to the maple tree's leaves, and to its syrup, that golden amber fluid that we sell at astonishing prices.

In the Middle Ages men used to think they could turn ordinary objects into gold. In Vermont ordinary objects like leaves and sap really do turn into gold, and Vermonters turn that gold into green, the kind bankers like.

Most of that money stays here, thanks to the maple. Maybe Ben and Jerry's could produce a seasonal treat called Maple Sundae, in tribute.

Or maybe we could tuck another observance into the Columbus Day weekend, a strictly Vermont holiday.

SEPTEMBER

We could call it Maple Appreciation Day, and we could celebrate it by being, just for a moment, as awestruck by what the maple is doing for us, as the flatlanders are by what the maple is doing to its leaves.

OCTOBER

The Last Color

Through all October's elder days
  A flush upon the mountain stays.

A trace, an echo for the eye
  Of color splashes just gone by
   To skate the wind in airy flood.

When all that's left of summer's cloak
  Is stubborn leaf on sturdy oak,

The golden glow of clustered larch
  Remains to make us think of March,
   . . . When men will cook the maple's blood

Beneath a plume of fragrant mists
  . . . And render gold like alchemists.

That Coat of Many Colors

In the Old Testament Book of Genesis the last chapters tell of Joseph, advisor to Pharaohs, pathfinder to Egypt, interpreter of dreams, and of course before all that, owner of a coat of many colors.

The tale says his brothers, jealous of that coat, sold the boy, stained his coat with lamb's blood, and used it to convince their father that Joseph had been killed by a wild animal. The saga went on, but the coat of many colors dropped out of the story and went missing.

I know where it is.

At least I know where it was last weekend. The coat of many colors was draped across the hills of Vermont. Those colors range from green to purple, by way of yellow, orange and crimson.

As the days get shorter, imagine Mother Nature confronting the forest trees as if she were a stage manager barking at a chorus line.

"Okay, all you trees, color up! Into your uniforms!"

The evergreens balk. "How vulgar!" they whine. "We don't do that."

The broadleaf trees obey of course, and put on their showtime makeup with varying degrees of enthusiasm.

You can almost hear the poplars and the birches going, "Aw, Mom!" as they turn a dutiful yellow. Some of the oaks just turn stubborn and go straight from green to brown, and then refuse to shed their leaves. Most of the other trees get into the act a bit more, with color displays ranging all the way up to orange. But they're all just a backdrop for the maples.

For sheer exhibitionistic exuberance nothing comes close to the maples. If you start with deep green and work your way up the color scale through lime and lemon and peach and orange to strawberry and apple to drop-dead crimson, there may be ten thousand subtle colors in between. And a big maple intent on showing off can display all of them, at the same time. I think they compete.

"Hey, look! I'm glowing!"

"Hah! You think that's garish, look at *this!*"

The entire northern forest becomes an orchestra performing the symphony of changing colors. The maples are the brass, and last week they were blaring, but it's a brief concert. On the higher hills there's already a touch of gray as bare branch tips emerge from beneath the coat of many colors. By next weekend those colors will be muted and the week after that they'll be gone.

Almost. Except for one last encore flash.

Remember that disdainful evergreen chorus? "*We* don't do that!" The pine and the spruce and the hemlock and the fir were all in that chorus, and so was the larch. The larch tries so hard to be an evergreen. It hangs out with them, looks like them, acts like them, and the pretense works as long as all eyes are on the maples.

But once those big leaves are gone, something odd happens to the larch. It colors up too, turns gold in fact, and then (gasp) drops its needles.

That is supremely embarrassing to the larch, and it stands around naked for the rest of the winter, trying to look dead.

But the larch does provide a service. It gives us something to hang onto as the season's colors are browning down. One last flash in the forest, one last echo of brightness to cup in the mind, and to hold there until spring.

Enfolding the High School Outcasts

On the coldest night of autumn there was a pep rally at my daughter's high school. There was no game. Instead it was an effort to build a tribal identity among the students and their adult supporters.

The kids who play on teams in the sports now in season competed with each other for bragging rights in the skits they put on to impress the judges and the fans in the stands.

While parents froze on the aluminum seats and the season's first snowflakes drifted in, the kids pranced and capered and cheered for each other. The football team was there, and so were the field hockey players, the boys' and girls' soccer teams and the cross-country runners.

These are the most active students in the school, and among them you will find next spring's Valedictorian graduate, musicians from the band and the jazz ensemble, student government reps and most of the drama club.

They seem to be involved in everything that happens in their insular world. And the adults who show up to cheer for those kids are also the most committed. They are the coaches and teachers and parents and Boosters' Club members who raise funds for so many of the extracurricular activities.

All the human resources that shape a positive high school experience were gathered on that field or in the stands for the pep rally.

The next morning the TV news was filled with horror. In Mississippi a high school kid is charged with stabbing his mother to death, and then taking a rifle to school and killing two classmates, one an ex-girlfriend. The principal said on TV that he was a quiet boy who had not drawn official attention because he "had not been a discipline problem."

In New Jersey a fifteen-year-old stands accused of sexual assault and murder in the death of an eleven-year-old who was selling candy door-to-door to raise cash for a classroom project. Somebody on TV said the kid they arrested did not mingle much, hardly ever left his house, and spent a lot of time at his computer.

I cannot be sure, but I suspect that neither of those boys ever went to a high school pep rally and danced onto the football field dressed as a California raisin hearin' it through the grapevine. My guess is that the two suspects were outside the main channel of life and of socializing in their schools, either because they never tried to be in the mainstream, or because they were expelled from it. Kids have an enormous tolerance for the kinds of eccentricity they define as benign, but they also have a tendency to shun the truly troubled as "too weird."

It would be foolish to suggest that the herd instinct among kids immunizes them from the kinds of outrages reported on TV that morning, or from a Columbine, or the outrage of the Virginia Tech massacre. It would be equally foolish to think that those who cherish solitude are somehow tilted toward tragedy.

But it does seem that in report after report on these incidents, the suspects in teenage tragedies are social misfits and see the world around them through a different and distorted lens. Look at the two Vermont teens who slaughtered a faculty couple at Dartmouth with a knife they'd bought on the internet. Sometimes, as in Virginia, the signs were clear and repetitive, but unheeded.

In Vermont and in other states school systems are starting to flag "apartness" as a signal that those kids require more alertness on the part of school administrators. They are starting special programs to enfold the students who don't have the social skills or the courage to push themselves into the mainstream. It's now recognized that the social outcasts can brood over slights, real or imagined, and that that brooding can fester into some awful form of lashing out.

The other side of that is to get the mainstreamers, the jocks in particular, to lay off the oddballs, the Goths and the freaks. No more looking the other way while the fringe kids get hazed or bullied or beaten up.

In schools that embrace such outreach programs it will be harder for administrators to say that nobody paid attention to a troubled kid because he was not overtly disruptive. Somebody should notice. Kids always know. They don't always feel compelled to tell adults what they know. Somebody should be aware that a teenager's reluctance to leave his home may be a danger sign, and should say so.

That's why building better relationships between the student body and its support groups is so vital. It doesn't mean turning every teen into a cheerleader or a linebacker or a goaltender or a clarinetist. But teachers, coaches, parents and administrators can be better positioned to distinguish between the odd and the ominous if they help create a vibrant school community, and then work to include the ones who may need help thriving in that community.

The Ides of October

Did you know that October has Ides, just like the Ides of March in the spring? It's the fifteenth. And yet the only Ides you ever hear about are the ones made famous by Shakespeare and that clutch of noble assassins who carved up Julius Caesar. "Beware the Ides of March" has become a verbal shorthand for good advice ignored.

Should we also beware the Ides of October? A glance at the historical record suggests probably not. Soviet leader Nikita Khrushchev was tossed out of office on October 15th, but his blood didn't run down the hallways of the Kremlin. They just told him to retire. That wasn't such a bad thing, except for the personal indignity involved.

On the same day in an earlier year, New York's LaGuardia Airport opened. The jury is still out on whether that was an achievement. And on another Ides of October, *I Love Lucy* first appeared on television. Piddling stuff compared to the Ides of March.

President Andrew Jackson was born on March 15th and so was country musician Roy Clark. The first escalator, the first blood bank and the first presidential news conference all date from the Ides of March.

The curtain went up on *My Fair Lady* in 1956 and down on the Ed Sullivan show in 1971.

I know why there's such an imbalance of important events between ones Ides and the other. There's a conspiracy against the Ides of October.

You want proof? Of course I've got proof, this isn't a conspiracy theory, it's a real conspiracy.

Here, listen to the words of the old pop standard, *September Song:*

"... And the days dwindle down to a precious few ...
September, November ..."

See there? The lyrics skip right over October as if it weren't even there. So does that mean the days of October aren't as precious as those that occur in the flanking months? Or is it that the songwriters simply have an aversion to a word as ugly as October?

It is, after all, quite a pleasant month. Hurricanes and thunderstorms diminish, the temperatures are temperate, the greenery is gaudy, and your favorite footballers may still have a decent season. Plus, it's not yet too cold to watch them play. And best of all it's Harvest Time, when the fruits of a year's labor are drawn from land sown with the faith of patient families.

So why don't the songwriters love October as much as they do other months? In April it rains a lot, it's Mud Season in Vermont, and my road pretends to be wet cement. And yet the songwriters just love April.

April Showers; April Love; April in Paris ...

See there? And there's June too. *June is bustin' out all over ...*

And so on for other months. May, July, September, even December.

Okay, the truth is that October is off the list because it has an ugly name.

Say it slowly. OC-TOE-BRRR. Where's the music in that?

A month with so much going for it should have a prettier name. Then maybe the songwriters would get inspired. It's hard to think of anything cute and cloying that rhymes with October.

But if we ever get that solved, there's always February. Now there's a challenge.

I Hear You, Brother Goose

Back in the old days, before CDs, before cassettes, before LPs and even before 45s, phonograph records were 78s. They spun fast, scratched easily and broke often.

In those days, more than half a century ago, a man named Frankie Laine sang exuberantly of big themes, of High Noon, and wagon trains, and the lure of the wild evoked by the honking of migratory geese.

Wild Goose, Brother Goose, he sang. *Which is best? A life of wanderin' or a heart at rest?*

In October in Vermont that question recurs, as the haunting call from above infiltrates the most sedentary of hearts. In Milton thousands of the big noisy birds go by on their way to the Chesapeake, to Albemarle Sound and other wintering grounds.

They pass high overhead along the shores of Lake Champlain, snow geese and Canadas in their separate squadrons. You can hear them coming long before you see the great Vee carved in the clouds as they arrow down to a warmer winter. They gabble incessantly, and the sound tugs at the grounded mind.

When Jack London wrote *The Call of the Wild* as the continent was domesticating most of its wild spots, he may have intended the title to evoke the entire allure of wilderness. But in every reader's mind that call took on a singular identity: the howl of the lonely wolf.

We have no wolves in Vermont these days, and our wild spots are few, protected, and their futures are always under debate. The call of the wild we hear is far from lonely. It is the gossip of the garrulous.

111

They make me want to go with them, to cut the sensible tethers of reality and responsibility, and just fly away. Not just to the warmer weather of Down-country, but to a destination much harder to find, and therefore much more attractive. It's the same goal that drove Gauguin to Tahiti, the same dream that gave us Shangri-La and Brigadoon. It's the notion of adventure, of discovery, of new vistas elsewhere, a place we always imagine to be better than here. So I listen to the bugling aloft and try not to hear the siren's song. I should think of hearth and home, of chores to do and commitments to keep.

Oh I hear you call me, Brother Goose, and I'm stirred to flight, even if oh, so briefly. I can't come with you, Brother Goose, but it's a comfort to know that you call forth the banked bit of wild in me. I will think about that while I move the plants indoors and stock the wood-box. Like other Vermonters, a non-migratory species for the most part, I will go into semi-hibernations against the coming chill. But Brother Goose, you remind me that the spirit need not be as tethered as the body.

Mister Bunnell's Halloween

Suppose someone concealing his identity should walk up to you and say, "Pay me now or something bad will happen to you."

That's extortion. It's a felony, and people go to prison for it.

When a three-year-old rabbit with a bag in her hand rings your doorbell and chirps, "Trick or Treat!" that's extortion too, but the kid doesn't know it yet. She'll learn.

By the time I was eleven my crowd had figured out that "Trick or Treat" was essentially a threat, and that the *treat* part was for little kids, and that we weren't little any more. Therefore we should do the trick part, if we could get it done without being caught. We all knew what "or else" meant in parental warnings.

So Jimmy and Jerry and OtherJimmy and I went in search of a mischief. Jimmy and Jerry were twins and OtherJimmy was their cousin.

We already had a victim in mind. We all wanted to "get" Mrs. Haughton. In school a generation is about four years. After that you're either forgotten or you're a legend. Mrs. Haughton was a legend.

Many generations of kids had a gripe with her because Mrs. Haughton kept all the softballs that sailed over her fence. Her property began about ten yards from the first-base line, and for left-handed hitters like me, batting became an exercise in trying not to hit a foul ball over the fence.

If you went over the fence after the ball, Mrs. Haughton would let out this ankle-biting dog, and she'd yell "Sic 'em!" The dog took his work seriously, and most of us had marks to prove he was good at it.

After a while we'd have to stop playing because Mrs. Haughton had all the softballs. Then she'd put them into a shopping bag and march over to sell them back to the school.

So Mrs. Haughton was a real target, but we never did her a mischief because of Willis. Willis Haughton was three years older than we were and a lot bigger. One of the filaments in his light bulb was missing. When we went by Willis in the fourth grade it was the year he began to shave. He was a biter too, so nobody messed with Willis, and we left his mother alone too.

That left Mister Bunnell. He was the principal and he paid Mrs. Haughton for all those softballs we were afraid to retrieve.

Besides, we owed him. Mister Bunnell had a steel hook where his right arm had been until a farm accident took it off, and he used to rap boys over the head with that hook to get their attention. It worked.

So Mister Bunnell was a legitimate target too, and he didn't have an ankle-biting dog. We had a plan. It was a secret, so we only told enough guys to be sure we'd get the credit when we pulled it off.

We certainly didn't tell Wretched the Third. Wretched's real name was Richard Pettegrew III, and he was a stool pigeon. His mother used to get out on her porch and scream, "Richard! You come home!" Some old men used to argue whether her voice carried farther than the air raid siren. He usually looked so miserable slinking home that Richard slid easily into Wretched. And then OtherJimmy found out in a Classics Illustrated comic book that England's King Richard III had been labeled a very bad monarch. That did it.

Wretched the Third he was, and he was a teacher-teller.

Just after dark on Halloween we got into Harry Mooberry's milking barn and forked a big gobbet of cowflop into a burlap bag. We were going to sneak that burlap bag onto Mister Bunnell's front porch, douse it with lighter fluid and set it on fire. Then we'd ring the bell and run for the bushes, and laugh like loons when Mister Bunnell would come outside and stomp out that fire.

But when we got there the big Oldsmobile was gone, and the house was dark except for the porch light, and there was a note on the screen door.

"Sorry, had to go out. Trick-or-treaters help yourselves." On the porch was a big bowl just full of Hershey bars, some with almonds.

Jimmy wanted to do the mischief anyway, but he was a bit slow, and Jerry had to point out that if we lit off the burlap and nobody came to put it out, we'd not only miss the fun of watching, but we might start a real fire.

Besides, if we took the candy we couldn't do the mischief. It wasn't "trick *and* treat," he said.

So we took some candy and threw the stinking burlap into Cooper's pasture and went home, thinking about how we were going to have to un-brag tomorrow to all those guys we had let in on the secret.

But as we were turning away I thought I saw the curtains wiggle in Mister Bunnell's living room, just a little.

And when Jerry got an "A" in deportment, which embarrassed him, I knew Mister Bunnell had been there, watching and listening, all along.

So we gave Wretched the Third a couple of noogies on the theory that if he hadn't spilled the beans he deserved it for some other tattle.

NOVEMBER

A Month of Two Minds

November is a schizophrenic time
Cause mostly it predicts a winter's woes.
The leaves and geese are gone and darkness grows,
And ponds chill down within a ring of rime.

The bears can barely bear it now, and hide
In rocky dens, and grumbly, fall asleep.
And then it snows; it's not yet skiing deep,
But grab the sled, perhaps enough to slide.

And now the autumn's other mood is strong.
Anticipate Thanksgiving's harvest feast
And revel in the season's joys released.
But don't forget that winter's really long.

A Tree Too Soon

When I worked in Boston there was a seasonal ritual that played out every year. It's probably going on there now.

On the morning after Halloween, at about sunrise, a tree arrives outside a huge urban complex that houses offices, shops, restaurants, apartments and a famous insurance company.

The tree probably looked noble standing in a Canadian forest. That's why it was selected. But now it looks diminished, tied down and lying on a flatbed truck with its branches snugged in by ropes, and looking like a restless patient strapped to a hospital gurney. The tree is a sacrifice to the Spirit of Christmas. Nova Scotia sends one here every year, perhaps out of gratitude that it avoided being annexed as a state back in the old days.

The next day the tree is standing again, frozen in place on an elevated platform that looks a little too much like an altar. Guy wires keep it from falling down.

Now there's a scaffold all around it and the big tree is getting the equivalent of a cosmetic make-over. People are fussing around it like so many apprentice hairdressers, lopping off branches that stick out a bit too much, offending someone's idea of what a perfect tree should look like.

Doesn't anybody tell these people that a perfect tree looks like a tree, and not like a Styrofoam cone?

Worse, they're drilling holes in the trunk in places where branches never grew, and they're jamming extra greenery into those holes, to supply what Nature forgot, as an old ad campaign had it.

And when they're through shaping this formerly beautiful tree into an improbable caricature of itself, they'll bring on the lights. So many of them that you won't be able to see the desecrated tree that supports them, just this huge cone of lights that can be made to shine blue, or blue and white, or red, or all together now. And yes there will be a star on the top. None of that is in place yet, but it's coming.

It's too soon. Not when I'm still in mourning for fallen leaves and flown geese. It's too soon for all that ho-ho-ho stuff. Hey, I'm still eating Halloween candy here.

One year the whole artificial confection blew down in a high wind, and I'm sure Mother Nature chuckled. I don't wish for that again. I'm not against the season to be jolly, just the remorseless marketing of it by people who seem to have lost all they ever knew, if anything, about the reason for having a tree, or for that matter a season, in the first place.

Did I miss something here? Aren't we still a few weeks ahead of Thanksgiving? You know, football, turkey, parades, harvest?

One season at a time, please.

In due course I'll go out to a neighbor's Christmas tree farm, in the snow if possible, and I'll cut my own tree, with advice and counsel from the family members who will help me trim it, without putting branches where they ain't.

But not now. Not yet. Not even this month.

Hunting Season

In Northern New England you can now see the forest for the trees. For the trees are naked and will stay that way for another five and a half months.

It is pleasant to walk in the woods these days; the air is crisp and the not yet rotted leaves crunch nicely underfoot.

But I'm not going to take that walk for a while. Deer hunting season begins on Saturday, or at least the rifle season does. Archers have already been out there, but there are relatively few of them, and they tend to look carefully at their targets before loosing their arrows.

Now it's rifle season, and for the next couple of weeks you had better not need a plumber or an electrician or any of the other specialists whose skills and services keep our civilization civil.

They'll all be out in the woods, thinking fierce and wearing orange to protect them from each other. The idea is that deer are color-blind but most hunters are not, and further that deer are not orange, and therefore orange is not a target.

In my Irish heritage the wearing of orange is a political statement I do not wish to make. But that's not the main reason that I don't go into the woods during hunting season.

The debate over whether deer hunting rewards violence is muted here in Vermont. The "Don't Shoot Bambi" argument doesn't thrive among people who understand that Bambi eats like a horse and breeds like a rabbit, and that starvation or cars would get him if hunters did not keep the herd in balance with the land's ability to support wildlife.

Besides, many Vermonters come from families in which venison has been a dietary staple for hundreds of years. Not so long ago, they point out, we were all hunters, dependent on our skill and patience to put food on our tables. Robin Hood and Daniel Boone, they say, became heroes for being very good at shooting deer and sharing their game.

The "Don't Shoot Bambi" crowd does not go into the woods during hunting season to protect the deer. It's not a good idea. Also, people at odds with each other in Vermont do not go hunting together.

They are honoring the local wisdom that says you do not accept an invitation to go deer hunting from someone you think may not like you.

That's because in northern New England you *cannot* get convicted for shooting someone with a rifle, outdoors, during deer season. "I thought he was a deer!" is the best of all alibis. That was affirmed several years ago by the Maine jury whose members acquitted a hunter who had shot a woman who was hanging out her laundry in her back yard and wearing white gloves.

A more recent case in Vermont ended in a mistrial when a jury could not convict a young hunter who fired into a tractor cab and killed another hunter who was sitting there waiting for the deer.

So I stay out of the woods and watch fall turn into winter. The calendar is wrong about when that happens, especially in the north. Winter begins long before the official date in the third week of next month.

Fortunately there are more holidays clustered in the winter, because that's when we need them most. In the gray of November, the month that has the most cloud cover and the least sunshine, it's important to have Thanksgiving sitting out there like a beacon in the gloom.

Finally there's the biggest holiday of all at Christmas, right after the shortest day of the year and probably set there deliberately to replace the old Celtic solstice celebration. After all, December 25th is the date of the Nativity by traditional agreement, and is not nearly as well established as the date of Julius Caesar's assassination four decades earlier.

And then we start over again with New Year's Day and Super Bowl Sunday, which is surely at least an informal holiday by now. All these occur while it is still bleak and dark and cold.

February brings Valentine's Day, devoted to candy and cards, and President's Day, co-opted by car dealers. And then it will be time to notice that the days are getting longer again. That's a long way to look forward, but you cannot go into the tunnel of winter without at least imagining the light at its end.

Lurking in the Woods

I'd like to put in a good word for the bears. Not "Da Bears." Not the Chicago football people whose identities are frozen in cartoonish personas labeled "Ditka" and "Butkus."

This is about the real bears, the black bears of New England, the ones we grew up learning to fear. Bears get a bad rap, and they don't deserve it all. Our traditions and folklore are filled with the notion that bears are bad news.

Consider Goldilocks. That cute little vandal breaks into the bears' home, rumples their beds and rearranges their chairs, and then eats their food. And when the bears come home and grumble at her, she runs away. The kid got off easy, and the bears get no credit for letting her go.

And remember the famous explorers speculating about the perils of the wild?

Lions and tiger and bears, oh my!
Lions and tiger and bears, oh my!

When I was little I knew there were no lions and tigers around, because we didn't have any jungle for a lion to be king of, and the tigers were off somewhere chasing each other around a tree and turning into butter.

But I was sure there were bears out there lurking in the woods. I wasn't quite sure what lurking was but I knew bears were good at it.

We're also taught that bears are really stupid. Silly old Winnie the Pooh gets caught between his brains and his breakfast, and breakfast wins, every time.

Poor Eeyore, something must not have agreed with him at breakfast. I shall just have to start eating from the beginning, and see where I went wrong.

And Joel Chandler Harris's Brer Bear in the Uncle Remus tales was a churlish lout with an attitude and a club.

Ah'm gon' knock yo' head clean off!

Native Americans are respectful of bears, who are considered symbols of power and strength. But in the Anglo culture, even when we say a bear is smart, we don't mean it.

Yogi Bear is smarter than the average bear . . .

But a lot dumber than Boo-Boo.

Having convinced our children that bears are big, dumb, bad-tempered and dangerous, we then try to counter that image with the gift of a teddy bear, every kid's cuddle pillow pal, and a Vermont industry of note.

Then we turn around and undo that effort by reminding those same kids that even teddy bears are not safe all the time.

If you go out in the woods today, you better not go alone.

It's lovely down in the woods today, but better to stay at home.

For every bear that ever there was will gather there today because

Today's the day the teddy bears have their picnic.

In a few days it will snow out in the deep woods. Most of the black bears are smart enough to live out there where they don't have to bump into *us* all the time. It will snow and the last of the acorns and beechnuts will be covered up. Food will become hard to find, and the bears are smart enough to stop trying. Instead they will find dens and sleep through until spring.

Now any critter that's smart enough to sleep through a Vermont winter is no dummy.

But in the spring they'll be out there again, and that's as it should be.

We need *something* out in the woods. We need the notion that something is lurking, whatever that is, to give us an extra edge of alertness when we're in the woods. That edge makes us see what's around us more clearly, even if we never spot a bear. We'll find that indeed it is lovely down in the woods today. Lions and tigers would be frightful, but bears . . . well, have a nice nap, fellas.

A Bowl of Rice, a Second Piece of Pie

Today we celebrate a holiday, a peculiarly American one, though somewhat related to the harvest festivals of other cultures. In northern Vermont it's hardly a harvest festival, because the growing season is so short that our harvest was finished long ago.

In about two hours I will sit down to a feast in the comfort of my home, and in the company of my family.

We will be renewing a tradition that began when New England was "New" England. It started as a celebration among people who had been tested in harsh conditions, and who, when they were sure they would survive, threw themselves a party and invited the neighbors.

We absorb a lot of grade-school mythology in learning about that first Thanksgiving. The Indians provided this and the Pilgrims cooked that, and they all sat down together to celebrate the bounty of Nature.

It's more likely that the event was a truce, an effort to keep the two cultures from drifting farther into distrust and antagonism. In the long run it didn't work, but the impulse to make peace, to break bread together in search of harmony, is still as strong and as noble as it was in the dawn of America's colonial past.

"Blessed are the peacemakers," we recite from a much older codex of virtues. The peacemakers must be patient, because their task is to neutralize the centrifugal forces that drive men and nations apart, and to instill in

126

their place the gravitational forces that draw people and communities together.

It is daunting work and we honor its practitioners for their courage, for their persistence, and for the incremental steps they achieve from time to time.

Menachem Begin and Anwar Sadat won the Nobel Peace Prize for orchestrating a significant pause in the ageless war between Arab and Jew. Yitzhak Rabin and Shimon Peres and Yasser Arafat won it later for a much less significant pause in the same conflict.

And yet the peace remains elusive and the giving of thanks for its blessings remains suspended.

In Northern Ireland the American mediator George Mitchell crafted the Good Friday agreement a few years ago as a framework for a governing authority that would empower the Republican Catholics without alienating the Loyalist Protestants. It still remains more promise than pact because truculence and suspicion remain strong in Ulster.

On this Thanksgiving Day my family and I will dine on roast turkey and all the traditional side dishes that make up the holiday menu. My children don't follow the news as closely as I do, and I might spoil their mood at that festive table by asking if anyone ever deserved a peace prize for, in Abraham Lincoln's words, binding up the nation's wounds.

If there had been a Nobel Peace Prize during the Civil War, would Lincoln have won it? In my town almost every man who could marched off to the distant battlefields of the Civil War. Well over two hundred of them left and well under two hundred came back. The names of those who did not are carved in stone. Headstones mostly, not monuments. In northern New England most of the monuments to the Civil War were raised much later by a generation looking backward for heroes.

In parts of this nation the wounds of that war are still unbound, unhealed. And so are those of more contemporary struggles among us, the civil rights movement, the Vietnam War, and the ongoing battle between privacy and conformity in the conduct of private lives.

We shout at each other and divide bitterly over public-policy questions, all the while losing trust in our public institutions. It's difficult to see what values have replaced our diminished confidence in politics, religion and journalism.

And yet for all the strife in America we are not a planetary hotspot. We are not wounded enough to galvanize the world to come to our aid. We are not beset by foreign peacekeepers with awesome weapons, by bureaucrats with food sacks, by international election-watchers, or by the solemn men who utter diplomatic gibberish at airports as they come and go in search of what's good for us.

Such people are busy elsewhere, and are needed. They're busy in places where the very idea of a Thanksgiving feast is beyond the mind's grasp.

So as we sit down in my house to potatoes and peas and gravy and stuffing and all the rest, there will be something else on the table.

We're going to cook a simple bowl of rice and serve it at a place where no one will sit.

It's a tradition.

It's a reminder to my family that while we feast in a prosperous and politically stable America, there are other places.

Places my children have barely heard of and cannot locate, where there will be no feast.

Not today, not soon, maybe just *not*. No feast. No peace. Not in the Holy Land, not in Afghanistan or Iraq and not in the turbulent ethnic clutter of Africa.

In many of those places the absence of peace equates to the absence of food. How much of a treasure would that simple bowl of rice be, if it were in one of those troubled lands?

In my home we will feast, and we will give thanks for what we have. But we will keep an eye on that bowl of rice, and we will consider the distance between that and a second piece of pumpkin pie.

DECEMBER

Act of Fear or Faith

An Act of Fear, or Faith, or Both,
Ice in autumn, stealthy, sneaking into ponds by night,
Giving way to solar melt a little later every day.
Ice invading, stubborn, sprouting in the chill
Until the day the warm won't come, and thereby winter will.

Daymelt ice, unlike the tide, leaves no track nor trace of its retreat.

But the mind scores what the eye records
And makes a case for the waning of the sun.

Where lies the case for its return, as autumn days deflate and darken?
My fire is a tiny sun; I grow it to fend off the dark and the cold.

"Can anything I've done have caused the sun to flee?
Can anything I do undo the drift and clothe my land again in green?"

Is it from the fragile etchings of early ice
That some ancestor bred the twins of fear and faith?

"If only I appease the spirits, the sun
Will once again bring heat and light and life."
But what spirits reign, what rites redeem?

Is it here we tap the source of art and myth?
Are totems carved to cage ideas, to tame the magic of images?

Where and when did men first chant the mantra of rebirth?
Utter words of faith as spells against the night?
Use the voice to compel the mind to deny the eye,
And thus the message of the ice?

131

DECEMBER

It must have been in northern lands
Where sunswing's price is clear and dear,
That decay of days was read as godly wrath.

Some Pict or Lapp or Inuit must first have said,
"Right there is where the sun turned 'round last year.
Let us pray to make it so once more."

Act of faith or act of fear, the doer doesn't care.
Just let the sun come back, and Polaris hold its place.

Apples in White Hats

The apples are staring at me through the window.

That sounds like the beginning of a story about a very troubled mind, but it's true anyway. And they're wearing little white hats. Like dunce caps, or wizard hats.

Now before you call in the guys with the strait-jackets . . .

There's an old apple tree outside my window and it makes stubborn apples. Too high to pick and too contrary to fall, they just hang there. There hasn't been a freeze severe enough to shrivel them, so they're still pretty plump, three months after they ripened.

Now last night it snowed, one of those magical early-season snowfalls right out of a Grandma Moses painting, with huge flakes drifting toward a reluctant touchdown, in still air.

This morning, each apple wears a conical snowcap, and it doesn't take much imagination to turn them into faces. Well, maybe it does. You have to be able to see Comanche scouts in the trees of a ridgeline, and Viking marauders behind a curtain of mist, if you're going to turn snow-covered apples into creatures.

I know who they are, these apples in hats.

They're Santa's guys, the elves who keep watch on children to make sure they deserve a visit from the Boss on Christmas Eve. There aren't any Santa-sized kids in this house these days, so I guess they keep watch on adults too.

I've known about Santa's guys ever since I was little. They were my early constraints against making mischief and cutting up, at least in the weeks between Thanksgiving and Christmas. Santa's guys were part of the framework of pressures that shaped a small boy's scruples. "The elves are watching, behave!"

It took a snowstorm to make me understand that they're still watching. How simple that is. I'm being watched, and so I'm on my best behavior.

But what about the rest of the year, when new snow and old apples don't make magic for the eye, and those little red faces aren't keeping score on me under those little white hats?

What then determines my conduct, or yours? Conscience, you say. But what is conscience except the awareness that actions have consequences? Most of the constraints against cheating, lying, stealing and meanness are internal. We shun such things because they offend our sense of right and wrong, our sense of fairness. When we say "That's not cool" we're expressing ethical discomfort and reaffirming a virtue-based value structure.

Are those values in decay? Do we lie and cheat and steal more than those who raised us? There's evidence that we've slipped some when we rush to find excuses for hockey thugs who sucker-punch opponents, for athletes who turn themselves into monsters and deny taking chemical potions, and for the politicians who will not reform the graft that stains the honorable craft of public service.

For all those people, I have an invitation. Come and sit by my window for a few minutes, and let Santa's guys look you over. They can tell what you are and they will tell the boss what to do about you. You do understand that when you leave that window, they will go with you. The snow and the apples only make them visible, but they do go with you, to help you resist the worst that's in you.

It's a way of applying the behavioral constraints of childhood to adult decisions. And that just might be worth trying, in this season and in all the others.

Uprisings and Peltings

It is cold and windless this morning, and the coffee mug warms my hand as I sit on a lakeside log and watch a thin sunrise try to paint color on a distant peak. It almost works, but nature's technicolor palette is out of season now, and the landscape is more and more shaded in the stark tones of the black and white scale. Just now gray is in play.

It lifts in wispy columns from the still water. A softly writhing blanket of silver gray moisture lies above the lake and dissipates at eight or ten feet above the surface. Exactly the same process is taking place in my coffee mug. Warm liquid is giving up its heat to cold air, and in the process is chilling down.

Lake Champlain stores up a lot of heat during the brief Vermont summer. The water temperature reaches the lower seventies, forty degrees above the freezing mark. By the end of December the lake will lose it all, and during a long still night soon after Christmas a thin skin of ice will form. Two weeks later it will be ice-fishing season, and the lake's roof will become two feet thick in the Inland Sea, and strong enough to support a railroad train.

In the boom and rumble as expansion cracks develop, my children will hear the echoes of summer thunderstorms. I will hear the older echo of big guns out beyond Da Nang.

What's going on this morning is an essential part of

that icing process, and is a textbook illustration of the physics of heat exchange in liquids and gases.

But it's far too fascinating to interpret only in scientific terms. When the mist erases distant shores, when it appears to move with purpose, might there be magic present?

How close *is* the link between image and imagination, between mirage and magic?

What lurks behind that shimmering curtain? The ordinary other shore or is it Otherworld? Do I hear a Celtic piper or is it just the gulls? Are these the mists of Avalon? Or will the stillness be shattered by the carved prows of Viking longships spilling horn-helmeted warriors onto the west coast of New England?

When you can't see the everyday reality the mind supplies a more enticing maybe. Yeah, I know, I've got to stop reading historical fiction.

But anything seems possible in the mists of morning.

Circles on the surface. Small hissing sounds and the bounce of white specks on the shore. The mood breaks as a spate of sleet hits the lake like spent shotgun pellets. We're out of Avalon now, back to the laws of physics. That warm moisture being sucked out of the lake is coming back cold and hard, as if to confirm one of our oldest folk sayings: what goes up must come down.

It's reassuring to note that in this give and take, as in most of its workings, nature is in balance. The mist does not obscure that fact even now, when falling leaves, retreating sun and fleeing geese provide sensory proof that the world is shutting down. It's not, of course, but the sight that meets the eye, the sound that greets the ear, the air that chills the skin all combine to suggest the end of things. Even so, I can say, "The sun will come up tomorrow."

That's no small act of faith, either for a red-dressed waif on a Broadway stage or for a down-vested apprentice elder sipping coffee on a log in the slowly spreading brightness of a December dawn.

Kitty Hawk Day

United Flight 422, now boarding at Gate 14 . . .

On any given day millions of people hear the distinctive sound of the transportation web that weaves the world together.

Su atencion, por favor . . . Aero-Mexico Vuelo 573 . . .

This is a good time to recall how important aviation is, because this December 17th is Kitty Hawk Day. In New York it's used as a conveniently non-sectarian date between Hanukkah and Christmas, so offices can have parties that don't offend anyone. But of course that's just a side effect.

It's more than a hundred years now since Wilbur and Orville Wright fulfilled a dream that began when men first envied birds.

They flew. Briefly and tentatively, but they flew.

Sixty years later I attended a milestone anniversary of that flight, at Kitty Hawk, North Carolina. The main attraction on that day was John Glenn, who the year before had done for the American Age of Space what the Wrights had done for the Age of Flight: started it, with his three orbits in the tiny space capsule *Friendship 7*.

That's now on display at the Smithsonian in Washington, where it's a centerpiece in the lobby of the Air and Space Museum. Visitors invariably say the scorched capsule looks too small and too frail to have done what it did; that is to take a man far into an implacably hostile environment, and bring him back again. The Wright Brothers' first plane is there too, but on that sixtieth anniversary there was a replica of it at Kitty Hawk.

DECEMBER

The country needed an uplift in December of 1963. We had just buried Camelot, and the war in Vietnam was not going well. And there in Kitty Hawk was an authentic American hero, as if to remind a sorrowing nation that glory is a counterweight to grief.

That day in Kitty Hawk the cameramen urged John Glenn to sit in what the newspapers of the day called "the operator's chair." He sat there for a few minutes, and grinned that grin, and said, "I don't see how they did it."

Those who built on the Wright Brothers' achievement, including Glenn himself, changed the way we travel and the way we wage war, and their names are still linked to their achievements. Perhaps never before had technology and exuberance been linked in such a grand adventure. And never before had the public been so fascinated.

Off we go, into the wild blue yonder . . .

Colonel Billy Mitchell and Captain Eddie Rickenbacker and Baron Manfred Von Richtofen.

Come fly with me, come fly away . . .

Charles Lindbergh and Wiley Post and Amelia Earhardt.

Fly me to the moon . . .

General Jimmy Doolittle, Colonel Paul Tibbetts, Chuck Yeager and Neil Armstrong.

I'm leavin' on a jet plane . . .

By now most of us are adjusted to a world made smaller by the giants of aviation. We complain about the cost of flying, and we suppress the fear of flying, especially after discovering that passenger jets can be used as flying smart-bombs.

But we think of ourselves as passengers, as a herd of people in a rush to get from here to there, willing to put up with bumpiness and inedible meals, if any.

So it's hard for us, flying public though we may be, to imagine the singular glory of steering something through nothing, of flying.

Wilbur Wright knew that feeling before anyone else. But maybe a Royal Canadian Air Force pilot said it better than anyone who ever flew.

Oh, I have slipped the surly bonds of earth
And danced the skies on laughter-silvered wings.

Sunward I've climbed, and joined the tumbling mirth
of sunsplit clouds,
And done a hundred things you have not dreamed of:
Wheeled and soared and swung high in sunlit silence.

Hovering there, I've chased the wind along,
And flung my craft through footless halls of air.

Up the long delirious burning blue, I've topped the
windswept heights with easy grace,
Where never lark or even eagle flew.

And while with silent lifting mind I've trod the high
un-trespassed sanctity of space,
Put out my hand and touched the face of God.

President Ronald Reagan quoted part of that at a memorial service for the Challenger astronauts in 1986.

John Gillespie McGee wrote it in 1941, before John Glenn became a pilot. It still works, even for passengers, in that moment when the jet leans back and lifts, to break that surly bond.

Feliz Navidad in Bethlehem

In 1868 a Boston-born Episcopal bishop, moved by the spirit of Christmas, published the words to a song of the season. His name was Phillips Brooks, and you learned his song when you were very young.

O Little Town of Bethlehem, how still we see thee lie. . .

Above thy deep and dreamless sleep the silent stars go by. . . .

Bishop Brooks never saw that little town, and wrote those words out of a vivid and pious imagination. He should have been right. Bethlehem ought to be a place of stillness, of quiet contemplation and spirituality. It's not. Worldly strife and gun-barrel politics ought to be kept at bay. They're not. Bethlehem seethes, along with the other communities of the West Bank.

The Palestinian-Israeli struggles continue to underscore the absence of peace in the birthplace of the Prince of Peace.

There are places on the earth where great tectonic plates push against each other, and those places are prone to natural earthquakes and volcanoes.

There are places on the earth where cultural plates push against each other, and those places are prone to civic earthquakes and eruptions. Bethlehem is one of those places.

Rudyard Kipling got it wrong. East does meet West. It's often contact by collision.

Islam against Christianity against Judaism. Democracy against monarchy and despotism. Oil against the absence of it. Free-market economics against government control.

All those cultural, religious, political and economic forces are in flux in the Middle East. Jerusalem is the epicenter of those conflicts, and Bethlehem is its side door.

The conflicts are so intense that the locals can't even agree on what the name means. In Hebrew it's *Beit Lechem*, the house of bread. In Arabic it's *Bet Lahn*, the house of meat.

It is an Arab town five or six miles south of Jerusalem, and built on the last ridge before the Biblical Wilderness falls away toward the Dead Sea to the east. On clear nights lights flicker in the Mountains of Moab, miles away in Jordan.

Back in the Seventies I was a reporter sent to cover Christmas at Bethlehem. It was considered a tough assignment because a physician named Luke told that story a long time ago, and nobody ever did it better.

In Bethlehem all roads lead to Manger Square, a huge plaza that faces the Church of the Nativity. There aren't many irreverent visitors to Bethlehem, but those are the ones who have labeled the plaza "Mangy Square" because of its unabashed commercialism. The original structure was built on Emperor Constantine's orders. His mother, St. Helena, had toured the Holy land in the Fourth Century. Guided by faith and locally kept tradition, she pinpointed the major sites of Christianity. The Nativity was here, she said, and there they built the church.

During the Middle Ages they had to brick up most of the main entrance to keep the pagans from riding their horses inside and disrupting the services, to say nothing of looting the place of gifts left by the pious.

The pagans don't do that very much these days, but the entry is still too small to admit a horse, just in case.

A few years ago the place became a fortress for Palestinian gunmen resisting the Israeli army, which re-imposed its control over Bethlehem as an Intifada heated up in the wake of yet another failed peace formula.

Inside, beyond the section of original brightly colored Byzantine floor mosaics, there's a stairway to a grotto under the main altar. Guides conduct tours to a tiny chamber where the light of candles illuminates lavish gold and silver furnishings. There's a silver star on the floor, where St. Helena said a tired carpenter once sheltered his laboring wife, and where a religion was born. Donations are solicited.

Outside, Manger Square is in the Jesus business, and is surrounded by the stalls and shops of merchants selling souvenirs, some guaranteed to be holy, to the Christians who come on pilgrimage to the site of the Nativity.

Mister, you want a piece of the True Cross?

Most of the merchants are Christians too, which confuses the Baptists and Lutherans and Catholics who see them in Arab dress and make faulty assumptions. Their ancestors made the same flawed assumptions during the Crusades and attacked everyone wearing eastern robes, Christians included.

The visitors bring their own visions of Bethlehem, visions indelibly set in their minds by illustrated childhood storybooks, and by Bishop Brooks' song.

When I was there one Christmas Eve in the mid-Seventies, pilgrims and sellers were haggling in English and French, and carols were being played in German over a loudspeaker system. All that competed with the crackling Hebrew coming out of walkie-talkie radios, as Israeli army squads patrolled against the annual Palestinian bomb threat.

Nobody seemed to notice the irony in that. Here were the Children of Abraham protecting the Lambs of God from the Sons of the Prophet. The Christian merchants of Bethlehem were just as restive as the Muslims, but they didn't do bomb threats, especially at Christmas. Bad for business.

Caught up in the swirl and babble of Manger Square that night were two small men with the stamp of the Andes on their faces and the blue berets of the U.N. peacekeeping force on their heads. They were members of the Peruvian battalion then stationed on the Golan Heights to remind the Israeli and Syrian armies to stay away from each other.

The soldiers on leave had come to Bethlehem for religious inspiration, and from the way they were shooing off kids trying to sell them olivewood crucifixes, they weren't finding it in Manger Square. An American wearing a package tour's name tag nodded to the two Peruvians and said, "Feliz Navidad."

That familiar phrase, in such an unfamiliar place, produced instant grins. After a short conversation in Spanish the soldiers drifted off toward the Nativity grotto, and the tourist's wife said, "You don't speak to strangers in Rochester."

"They weren't really strangers," he said. "They came here for the same reason we did, and they were just having a little trouble with the clutter."

Bishop Brooks, every once in a while your little town shows a flash of living up to your image of it.

Yet in thy dark streets shineth the everlasting light. . . .
The hopes and fears of all the year are met in thee tonight.

They're Back!

Becoming an ancestor is a gradual process. There are kids, and then they grow up. By the way the empty nest is a pretty nice place to live.

There are weddings, and there are births, and you hope they occur in that order.

Now the nest is far from empty, and the dooryard is cluttered with cars from Away.

The kids are back, with attachments, just for the holidays. We feel lucky they're all here, because the attachments have families of their own, and they wanted to host the kids as well.

One of the subtle blessings of a durable marriage is that for the kids, it simplifies the number of possible answers to the question: "Whose house will we visit this Christmas?"

On our side at least, there's relative simplicity. Just one ex, and she's been out of the mix for decades, and is not a factor in decisions over where to spend Christmas.

So here come the kids, all grown. One arrives from Boston, where she went to college, and where she works trying to bring some order and stability to the lives of schizophrenics in a state-operated half-way house. We worry about that, but if she does too, it doesn't show through a sunny disposition.

There's a sister, fifteen years older, and even sunnier. She's one of the new moms who have cluttered up my house with plastic baby containers of one kind or another.

Most of these things didn't exist when the last generation was teething. There is a bouncer, and a big plastic ring with a seat in the middle and a series of slots where moms can stick diversions, all of them designed to make the baby brighter. We'll see.

Baby strollers, if you haven't noticed, are a lot bulkier and a lot more expensive than they used to be, even if they do double as car seats, which were a lot smaller and cheaper when these new parents were little.

So there's a thirty-something new mom and a twenty-something new mom, and their babies are about four months apart.

This is the first Christmas we've got them both here, and it requires some adjustments.

We trimmed the tree, and then had to untrim a lot of it so little hands wouldn't grab at decorations designed precisely to attract the eye.

All kinds of stuff comes up off ground level as part of the baby-proofing process, and now the house is barren from about waist-level on down. It looks a little like trees in a pasture, nibbled naked up to about four feet off the ground.

I grumble at the un-decorating, but they know I don't mean it. I'm supposed to grumble. It's part of my curmudgeonly grandpa persona.

What I'm really thinking is that it may be many years before we go through another Christmas in this house without having either a crawler or a swelly belly around to spice up the celebration. I hope that comes true.

We're restricting the distribution of presents to focus on the babies, and in fact that's what the entire week is about.

When you're an ancestor the real meaning of all this togetherness is easy to experience but hard to verbalize.

DECEMBER

I think watching grandchild One take toys away from grandchild Two, and then watching the moms come to quell the resulting storm, is worth tons of words.

As parents, we sit back a bit after the bustle of arrivals and settling in, and evaluate. We think we've done the launching thing pretty well. Maybe we didn't do everything right, but it's now clear we didn't screw up either.

Of course, as Vermonters, even as recovering Flatlanders, we can't say that, especially to them. We don't even say out loud the phrase that echoes in our minds as they arrive, the one their grandparents used in countless welcomes: "My, how you've grown!"

Now the growth is internal rather than vertical, but to us it's just as visible and just as real, and plenty to be thankful for. And then there are the babies.

Does every grandparent feel the same? Is it like this for all of us, sitting quietly and watching an explosion of energy animate a house that usually runs at percolate rather than at boil?

Nobody tells the young there is such a dividend, or if they do the young don't listen.

It's easy to see the toll that age takes on elders. Things sag, and change shape and color, and the body slows. Conversations tend toward embellishments of, "the doctor said. . . ."

That's what the kids notice. Not that it will ever happen to them, of course, but they see it happening to us and to our still-living parents.

But look. The little guy who can't quite walk tries so hard to keep up with his cousin who can walk, barely. Every step is an adventure for her, and there's a reason why potty training doesn't begin until age two. That diaper makes very good padding for sudden losses of balance.

They are the future, my future, and I can't get enough of them.

I will tell them of my grandfather, and stories of the brave and hungry people two generations before him who came to this country because the potato would no longer feed them in Ireland.

I will say that my grandfather told me that you are never really dead until your descendants forget your name. Then I will tell them his name, and hope that when they are old they will tell mine to another set of little kids.

Oh, and one more thing to be grateful for.

In a few days, they'll all go home.

JANUARY

Toasting Tomorrow

Almost every year there's a new James Bond film timed to grab the lucrative holiday market for movies. The old formula still works: suave hero, beautiful women, imaginative gadgets and lots of action, preferably with high explosives involved.

But long before Sean Connery first drawled "Bond, James Bond," another British agent already had a grip on the American fancy.

Between the World Wars and into the Cold War there was British Intelligence agent Tommy Hambledon, described as a short spare man (most unBond-like) with an air of authority about him. He was popular enough to star in a dozen hard-cover thrillers. He shot the really bad guys "neatly through the head" as the text often had it, and usually he goaded lesser villains into doing something stupid in such a public way that the not-very-bright police would reel them in.

Tommy Hambledon's first two adventures were called *Drink to Yesterday* and *A Toast to Tomorrow*. I pulled those volumes off a dusty shelf while trying to keep a New Year's resolution to weed my life, and it seemed to me that we do both those things on New Year's Eve. We lift a glass either in relief or in regret over what's gone by, and we hail with hope whatever's to come.

The Romans even invented a god for that sort of thing, and gave him two faces, one looking forward and one looking back. His name was Janus, and we are now in his month.

First Night in Burlington and in Montpelier, Rutland and St. Johnsbury this week was one of those crossover events that Janus might have loved, where you look both ways at the same time. Music, fireworks and food in an alcohol-free environment, and finally that pause at the midnight moment to count down, blow horns, kiss partners and shout, "Happy New Year!"

And then of course, the song. To my taste it's the Guy Lombardo version with all those saxophones gliding through the notes of *Auld Lang Syne* on a tinny old radio that brought in the voice of Ben Grauer standing in the middle of the tumult in far-off Times Square.

First Night in Burlington is better. The celebrants here don't look so desperately in search of whatever it is they didn't find in the year just ended, as they do in New York.

It's better here, but not the best. The best, a very personal best to be sure, was my grandfather's house on New Year's Eve. He was a sturdy old man, sharp of nose and chin, and when I was small I thought he looked a lot like the newspaper caricature of the Old Year, welcoming the baby New Year in a diaper and sash. He was also sharp of mind and tongue, which makes me miss him still, especially on New Year's Eve.

He reveled in the occasion; it was an excuse to fill his home with friends and laughter. After the midnight countdown and the horn blowing and whooping, he would command a moment of silence. He'd take my grandmother's hand and recite to her and to everyone else a verse of his own making, on the passing of another milestone. Here's the one I still recall.

We've blown our horns and sung Lang Syne.
Now here's a toast of my design
To make the most of each tomorrow,
And hope it brings more joy than sorrow.

See, that's what New Year's Eve is for.
It's just a pause for keeping score.
This year my life's in extra innings;
It's time to balance loss and winnings.

A time to change, to say, "Yes dear,
I'll be a better man this year."
But wait a minute. I've been thinking.
Too much reform and too much linking

Of my well-being with "Thou shalt nots."
That won't cure my liver spots.
My pipe is out, my glass half empty,
And you're not even looking tempty.

If that's old age, I'm bearing up.
Just look what's left inside Life's cup.
While it no longer runneth over,
Still tastes of honey, smells of clover.

My grandfather's toast to the New Year. Every year
it fits me a bit better. Next year I think I'll gather some
friends in my house . . .

Cold Enough To Mention

The Southern members of my family call on days like this.

"How cold is it?"

"Well, the snow is squeaking."

That doesn't tell them much, but it's the opposite of "so hot you can fry an egg on the sidewalk." We don't say that in Vermont.

These cousins are the ones who call in April to say their azaleas are lovely this year. I say that's nice, and go out and chop ice dams on the roof.

I have azaleas too. They bloom in June, and seem apologetic about it.

In North Carolina it does snow from time to time. The cable news will have a story from Charlotte, showing cars doing ice-dancing moves that usually end abruptly. The pretty face will smirk and say that driving is an adventure in the Carolinas today, then turn quickly to the latest celebrity scandal.

In North Carolina the snow is invariably heavy and wet and instantly slushy.

They have no idea. What can you expect from a place where sugar maples won't grow?

In school I learned that the Eskimos have eighteen words to describe different kinds of snow, and later I learned that the Eskimos don't like being called Eskimos any more. They're Inuit now, and they live in Nunavut, which is most of what's between Greenland and Alaska, including Hudson's Bay, and north of where other people live.

154

I wonder what words the Inuit use to describe snow that squeaks when you walk on it. When you get squeaky snow, then it's cold, y'all cousins.

Mark Breen is the Fairbanks Museum weather guy whose "Goood Morning!" has started morning weathercasts on Vermont Public Radio for almost 20 years. He says snow squeaks at about five degrees above zero, and from there on down.

It does that because it's freeze dried. When the air gets that cold, it's usually dry, and it sucks moisture out of the snow on the ground. When you step on it, it compresses loudly.

That's a significant marker on the Vermont scale of cold, because it takes squeaky snow to get the RVs talking about cold. Real Vermonters zip the sleeves back into their down vests when the snow squeaks, and layer up their clothing to about five between skin and chill.

The weather geeks on TV are hyping up the cold, because that's what they do. "How cold is it going to get tonight? We're talking about serious Brrr factor here, folks, stay tuned for the *awesome* numbers!"

Cold air is thicker than warm air, so maybe there's more oxygen in it. Maybe that's why a spell of sub-zero days will get the old RVs to yarning about the old days, when it was *really* cold.

It takes about a generation for a serious cold snap to migrate from history to legend, goosed along by stories that begin, "Why this ain't cold. I remember when . . ."

There's a time for those stories. They're mothballed in the summer and they slumber until the bears pack it in for the season. Two years ago those stories never came out at all. There wasn't much ice and there wasn't much snow, and what there was never squeaked. No nights below zero and green grass in early April. It was unnatural, and nobody talked about the cold. It never got cold enough to mention, never passed the squeak mark.

This year it's different. We've had strings of days when it never got above zero in the daytime, and an inch or so of snow every day. About a generation from now a new story will begin:

"Why, this ain't cold. I remember back in Ought Three and Ought Four, it was so cold the Republicans in Vermont were all worried."

And the listener is supposed to ask, "Why was that?"

"Well they'd all promised the White House that Howard Dean was nothing to worry about. They said, 'He'll get elected when Hell freezes over!' An' Jeezum Crow, he sure had 'em checkin' their thermometers for a good while there."

When the Neighbors Hibernate

We have neighbors up the hill. She's a teacher and he's a psychologist. They built their home themselves up on a knoll where they have a breath-taking view of Lake Champlain's Inland Sea.

We see a lot of those neighbors in the summertime, down by the lake.

In the winter I'm aware of them by the light gleaming out from their house, and they know I'm here by the smoke rising from my chimney. There's a footpath up that hill, and those lights aren't far away, but somehow this season discourages contact. In the winter, a sort of semi-hibernation sets in, a clinging to the hearth.

It's not isolationism or withdrawal. We think nothing of driving ten miles to a basketball game or twenty to a movie, or even farther to one of those unVermont big stores that sell everything. A Vermont store is a little one that sells everything. And closer to home a brisk walk that brings the breath out in steamy plumes is fun, and fittening. 'Fittening' is a homemade word and so the computer underlines it in red as it would to note a mistake. Fittening is the opposite of fattening. I heard an old Vermonter say that splitting wood is fittening, and it is.

He's a thoughtful man of many seasons, and I must ask him why the winter seems to shrink sociability. After all, the neighbors up the hill don't growl and snarl when it gets cold; it's just that we don't see each other very much.

The New England poet Robert Frost was living in southern New Hampshire, in Derry, when he gave

157

us his famously unimaginative farmer neighbor who insisted while mending his wall, that good fences make good neighbors. When Frost wrote that, before World War I, southern New Hampshire was a lot less like Boston than it is now, and a lot more like northern Vermont. So I think I know that wall-mender. At least I know how he thinks.

Robert Frost specified that he had that walk-'n-talk with his good neighbor in the spring. They most surely did not go out in January to improve their boundary line and their mutual respect.

Maybe it's January that make good neighbors. Maybe the pulling-in is a socially necessary mechanism. Maybe it's January as much as a well-mended wall that keeps us from treading on each other's turf, from getting on each other's nerves, and from defining each other's idiosyncrasies as idiocies. Maybe it is January.

Thoughtful Vermonters have suggested that January seems longer than it really is, because the holiday excitement is over, because it truly does get cold and because the nights are fifteen hours long and the days only nine, although that does begin to improve by the end of the month.

Do you suppose that even the ski resort people get a bit weary of tree-cracking cold and the fourth snowfall of the week?

Nah. And if they did they'd never let on. The ski people, no matter how much snow they have, worry that something will make all those people from Away (any place outside Vermont) stay away, and not come here to buy neon clothes and high-tech sticks to make falling down more dangerous, all in the name of physical fittening for them and economic fattening for us.

We don't talk about this very much, but there are people here who don't like cold weather. We don't say so because recovering Flatlanders (people from Away who now live in Vermont) are usually fixated on being hardier than anybody, and they would never admit freezing, no matter what.

And as for the real Vermonters, the multi-generational natives weaned on Holstein milk and maple syrup, I've noticed that very few of them complain about things that do not respond to chiding. Like the weather, or the stones that fall off that wall every winter, as the hunters and the frost-heaves have their way with the stones in it. They may not like the annual mending wall ritual, but they do not rail against gravity, or other forces of nature.

Some distant day when the tundra is softening and the hillsides run with meltwater, I will meet my neighbor along the line between us. There is no wall on that line, and I almost wish we had one, but anyway I will say, "How was the winter?" and he will answer, "Not too bad." He always does. Not too bad to bear, and not so bad as to bear mention. Not too bad, he says. I think that means pretty good but the Vermont in him keeps him from saying that. "Not too bad" is as good as pretty good gets, in Vermont-speak.

Road Warriors

You become aware of the sound in the middle of a night when the falling snow has muffled all other noises. It sneaks into your ear and then grows into a roar, punctuated by bangs and rattles.

The road crew is out tonight, plowing snow and spreading salt or sand.

In our smaller towns, you know who's up in the high cab of that Town truck. On my road it's usually Chickie Deslaurier, scraping down to the dirt and trying to keep the sidewing blade from taking out a mailbox or two. He's been doing it for years. He drives the grader too, when the road gets holey in the spring and summer, and puts up with people calling him Chickadee.

I don't see Chickie Deslaurier very often, or Ralph Martucci or Bruce Travis or any of the other men who keep the town's roads open. When I do, it's usually at a Selectboard meeting where they try to pressure the board to increase their pay or their benefits. That often happens in the wintertime when their work is most visible.

The town road crews and their state counterparts keep Vermont open in the snow season. They make it possible for the school buses to travel the highways and rural roads in relative safety. They provide a sandy carpet over the ice so the retired couple down the road can make their daily run into the village.

When I hear the plow at 3:55 on some snowy morning I don't jump out of a warm bed and run outside to give Chickie Deslaurier a grin and a "thumbs up." He'd think I was crazy. He already does, because I'm a Flat-lander and I built a house that's bigger than he thinks I need. But I do appreciate what he and his colleagues do, even if it's hard to find a proper way to say so.

When the ice came a few winters ago, the road crew was out early and often. And when the trees cracked and came down, they worked with chainsaws as often as with sand and salt. Snowplow drivers tend to be guys who have a lot of useful skills.

The service they provide is, quite simply, mobil-ity. And we got a lesson about how important that is in the year of the ice storm, when we didn't have any mobility.

We didn't have any phone service for a while, either.

And we didn't have electricity for quite a long time. Precisely how long varied from place to place, often depending on how quickly the road crews could clear the way for the linemen to get at the ice damage. It was a time to notice that we've become so dependent on electricity that any power outage is quite a long time, because of the quite a few things we can no longer do.

I can't pump water out of my well or into my septic tank without electricity. I can't heat my water because it's done through the furnace, which requires electricity. My workplace, a desk with a computer on it, goes back to being cluttered furniture.

I can't wash clothes, make toast, fry bacon, dry hair, bake potatoes, pump gasoline or write a story, because the kilowatt isn't ready to help me.

All those things *can* be done without electricity, and I know how to do most of them. But I'm out of prac-tice, and my kids have had no experience at all in getting by without the magic that comes out of the slots in the wall.

Now, thanks to a storm that dropped an inch of ice across the region we've all had a lesson in how fragile are the links in the chain of assumptions that we make in choosing to live forty miles from where we work, or in choosing to work at home and stay connected by computer.

The lifestyle we have evolved requires, demands, that the roads be open, that the phone works, and that there be electricity in steady supply. Together those things are called infrastructure, and they allow us to dominate our environment. Ice exposes the frailty of that domination, and the road crews represent our determination to restore it.

Snow does not deny us mobility, it just slows us down a bit. Ice is different, and has far more power to disrupt and destroy. It took a long time to restore power to some of the hard-hit areas, and the first step in that recovery was the clearing of the roads.

Unclog the arteries. Deny the storm its ability to isolate us from each other. If that means cutting away bent birches and broken pines, so be it.

The road warriors went to work and got it done. That's what they do in towns all over northern New England.

How many of us can rest after a long day's work and say in total honesty, "I have done something truly useful today." The road crews can. It must be very satisfying work.

Real Vermonterhood

Last weekend the Vermont highways were really crowded, especially the southbound lanes on Interstates 89 and 91. On Sunday afternoons it's as if somebody pulls a giant drain plug, and half of New York and most of Boston come spilling out of the nicer parts of Vermont. There's a tide of homebound cars all wearing ski racks over license plates that say "We're from Away."

Vermonters are pretty good at getting people from Away to come here and spend money on non-essentials; looking at dead leaves, buying images of black-and-white cows, and buying gallons of boiled tree juice. Vermonters are especially good at getting people from Away to come here to stand on high-tech sticks and practice falling down in deep snow.

Maybe skiing is so popular because its addicts feel compelled to spend money on expensive equipment and day-glo clothing, and a lot of that money stays in Vermont.

Our other winter sport is not so popular, perhaps because you don't need expensive stuff. It's sort of a northern border secret practiced all across the upper edges of America. You can start a hot-stove argument in any short stop in northern New England over where this sport's most avid fans are to be found, and in every one of those gas station/stores, somebody will have a story about the best who ever lived, and everywhere he was a local guy.

Come on, I'll take you with me into the secret, but watch your step, it's slippery here.

163

Okay we're standing on the roof of Lake Champlain, getting ready for the first scene in an irrational act. Here, hold the augur. I've got to shovel the snow off the ice so we can drill it.

Yeah, that giant corkscrew looking thing. Just twist the handle. Look how it churns up a neat collar of shaved ice. Too bad there's absolutely no demand for shaved ice in Vermont in January.

There, we've got a column through about eighteen inches of ice, big enough to push a football into, or pull a fish out of.

That's the idea. This is ice fishing. You are participating in an ancient cultural ritual of the North. Aren't you thrilled? Not chilled, *thrilled*. You're not allowed to be chilled, even though there's a twenty-below wind chill riding on a breeze that's coming straight out of Canada, which is only thirty miles away. Never mind the cold, it perfects the experience we're having.

What you do is, you sit on an upside down plastic five-gallon bucket and you drop a line down through that hole. On the end of the line, hiding the hook, there's a gobbet of colored plastic designed to look like a fish eye. Real Vermonters say the perch just go crazy over that fake fisheye, and jump on the hook.

Okay down there, I'm ready.

Hmmm, there seem to be pauses between the thrills in ice fishing.

So we've got time to chat, and to think. Thoughts like *What am I doing here?*

I don't know about you, but I'm laying the groundwork for my remote descendants to claim Real Vermonterhood. You see, I can't be a Real Vermonter. I wasn't born here. My kids can't either. Same reason, even though they got here pretty young. It's like running for president. You have to be born here to qualify.

But in Vermont it's even more restrictive. Your parents have to be born here too, at a minimum.

Come on, fish!

You know, Howard Dean could become governor without ever being a Real Vermonter. Madeleine Kunin, too. Jeezum Crow, she was even born in Switzerland.

I don't have any grandchildren yet, but when they're born here in Vermont, they won't be real Vermonters, even if my kids marry natives.

But my great-grandchildren will qualify, unless the RVs change the rules again.

Seventh-generation Vermonters get to do that, but they tend to avoid meetings, so they probably won't bother.

Never met a seventh-generation Vermonter? Haven't been here long, have you? They're everywhere, and they're not shy about letting you know they're RVs, and you're a Flatlander, even if you live here for 90 years and have the accent down cold.

The accent? Pretty easy, really. Just put an "O" sound in front of every "I" or "Y." As in "Oy'm going out to roide moy boike." Oh yeah, and don't pronounce any "T" in the middle of a word. Use a glottal stop instead, like "Wear your mi' 'ens to keep your hands warm." Or the name of the town we're in. It's not Milton, it's Mil'in. There you go.

Okay, so here we are sitting a hundred yards off the Mil'in shore of Lake Champlain, and my feet have just divorced the rest of me, and my lips don't work any more and the fish don't like gobbets of colored plastic today.

But really, all this is worthwhile. With this exercise in minimal satisfaction, I tell myself that I'm putting the necessary lore and legend into place. Some child two generations unborn will be able to look out over the lake at the end of this new century and say, "Yup, my grea' grandfather the Fla'lander, he used to go ice-fishing right out there."

So I'm doing this for posterity, banking up credentials against the time when there will be a test of Real Vermonter.

Oh, and when we're finished having fun out here, and get thawed out, there will be another test. This year I will be invited to slog through melting snow and freezing mud, to carry heavy buckets of sap, so some Real Vermonter can boil it down into maple syrup. That happens in March. You want to go along? Bring your mi"ens.

FEBRUARY

Cabin Fever

There has always been a sense of restlessness associated with being shut in. Prison inmates describe that feeling as being stir-crazy. The northern winter imposes a milder version of the same thing. The urge to move, to be physically active is still strong in us, even when the climate makes it hard to scratch that itch. Maybe that urge helps us explain the allure of skiing, snowboarding, snowmobiling and all the other activities we embrace when the weather is so bad that bears and other sensible creatures snore it off.

We can't do that. Oh, we try on the occasional lazy weekend when the honey-do list is short and the football games aren't very good. But those lazy weekends don't come along very often because we keep inventing special days to shield us from the reality of the season. Valentine's Day, President's Day and even Groundhog Day are designed as diversions.

Can you imagine that at any other time of the year the nation would stand still to see what happens, when

A garden-gobbling critter by the name of Phil
Emerges on the Second from a Pennsylvania hill?

There is a pageant there that beast and men portray.
They gather in the dawn, with each his role to play.

See, here the scribes festooned with lens or tape or pen,
And there the locals clot, those sturdy grizzled men.

The sun comes up and so does Phil. The cameras whine
And now the sages come to speak their only line.

"Six more weeks," they say, and squinty eyes hide grins.
Such earnest noting of a guess, at when the spring begins.

They're right, of course. The ice grows thick and snow falls fast.
I feel confined, it's Cabin Fever time. How will I ever last?

Such a tradition could never thrive in Vermont. After all six more weeks takes you only to the Ides of March, not one of history's lucky days.

And besides, in Vermont it's yet another six weeks from the middle of March until the leaves pop out in early May. And finally, while native Vermonters sometimes identify themselves as woodchucks, not one of them would trust that rodent to forecast the weather.

The truth is, Cabin Fever is not as bad as it used to be, in the days before electricity offered escape via the radio, or the TV or rented movies.

This era offers too much diversion for real malaise to set in. But think of the earlier days that spawned the phrase, when winter reduced the world to the tiny orbit of cabin, woodpile, outhouse and barn. No cable TV, no phone and no escape to Florida.

Even with our modern advantages, we still get twinges of one of the first manifestations of stress ever to become an expression in our language.

Is "going Postal" another?

The human mind chafes at enforced isolation. That's why solitary confinement is considered in some quarters to be a cruel and unusual punishment. So a person's state of mind is not likely to be nourished by the limitations winter imposes on social beings.

Juries are occasionally sequestered, quarantined, cut off from outside influences while they hear and decide important cases. Ex-jurors report feeling hemmed in, confined, constrained and therefore discontented. They are describing the symptoms of cabin fever.

Vermont psychologist Terry Dutton is a veteran of many winters in isolated settings. He says monotony is the enemy and that activity is the antidote for cabin fever.

If it's not motion of the body, then motion of the

mind will do. After all it was during the long northern winters that our ancestors trudged through those heavy, slow-moving 19th Century novels. And surely it was during the winters that the most striking achievements of Yankee ingenuity were generated, from the humble clothespin to such complex ideas as public education, and local government by Town Meeting.

So fight off cabin fever. Read a book, a modern one will do. Do a jigsaw puzzle that forms an image of a place you'd rather be just now. Write something. Paint something. Carve something. Bake something. Create something out of the enforced idleness of the body.

And if you're in doubt about how to get started, Terry Dutton says ask a kid. Any age will do.

There's Nobody Named Feb

When I was a kid the word "hate" was leached out of my vocabulary. Or so I thought. Whenever I told my brother I hated him, my elders would sit me down and explain that while he was indeed a pesky nuisance, that wasn't a hateable offense. And I should find another word.

I tried "despise," but "despise" is not a very good verbal hammer.

I was also, um, persuaded, that I did not hate the fourth grade teacher, the dog that chased me, or asparagus. "It's all right not to like those things but you can't hate them."

All right, lesson learned. I now know that hating is a symptom of emotional immaturity.

Having said that, I hate February. So there. I know hating allows bias and bigotry to distort good judgment, but consider February.

It begins with Groundhog Day, an observance devoted to predicting how rotten the rest of the month is going to be. And the prophet for that forecast is a fat rodent who specializes in harvesting gardens before the people who plant them think the crops are quite ripe.

Then you need other holidays to divert your attention from brooding over just how unpleasant this month really is.

170

We have President's Day, which honors George Washington and Abraham Lincoln. Each of our greatest presidents used to have his own holiday, on his birthday.

No more. They've been blended into the nearest convenient Monday. Some honor.

You celebrate the legacy of our presidential icons by going out and buying a car made in Japan. That's what the car guys tell you on TV, happily ignoring the fact that Japanese Jeeps didn't exist when either leader lived.

"Only three more days in our giant President's Day Sales Event!" they yell. Somehow a good old sale has become a Sales Event. Who knows why?

Last year a local Ford dealer even made a tasteless reference to Ford's Theatre in Washington.

By the way, nobody ever implores you to buy a car to honor the spirit of William Henry Harrison, also born this month. That's because Harrison gave a three-hour inauguration speech in the rain, and caught cold. Tippecanoe, achoo, achoo. A month later John Tyler was president.

And let's not forget Valentine's Day. It's named after an early saint whose distinction as a martyr was that Roman archers turned him into a human pincushion. Maybe that's the origin of that nasty little cartoon cherub who goes around shooting people with arrows to make them realize they're in love.

Valentine's Day belongs to the flower sellers and the candy man and the greeting card people. Their idea is, "Make a nice gesture toward someone special in your life." Well, if you do that only on Valentine's Day, there won't *be* anyone special in your life.

Now consider the name: February. You can't even pronounce it. Who tucked that "R" in behind the "B" anyway? Feb-brew-airy. Right. How often do you hear it that way?

Feb-you-airy. Feb-wary. And for those with the British speech defect, even Feb-bry.

FEBRUARY

Can you imagine a mother naming her daughter February? Look, there's lot of Aprils and Mays and Junes running around, and even some Springs and Summers. And I read the other day that some cruel parents named their daughter "Wynter Snow." How cutesy. How sad. I've got nothing against calendar names. After all there was a guy in *Lonesome Dove* called July Johnson, and one of the heroes was called Augustus.

But Februarius? No thankius!

It's really the Febr part that annoys the ear, but the airy part is suspect as well.

Think for a moment of the last four months of the year, when the temperatures are cooling down to winter. All their names, appropriately, end with "brrr." But now, when it's really cold and miserable, we have two months that end in "airy." Calling January and February "airy" is what the Brits call understatement.

The name comes from Februa, an ancient purification ritual the Romans used to perform in the middle of the month. Everybody knows the Romans soon tired of purity, but the name stuck. I can't imagine that for two thousand years nobody's been able to improve on it.

Now it's time. Let's purify February. We have a great fertile language that spawns dozens of new words every year. Car makers and medicine makers can come up with catchy names that mean nothing, to label their products. Let's enlist their namers to abolish February and come up with something that's a bit less ugly on the ear.

But think fast, because the sole grace of February is that at least it's short, even in Leap Year.

To Fly or To Abide

This has been a troubling week for transplanted Vermonters. We are a people apart here, also called Recovering Flatlanders, or more dismissively, people from Away.

We're the ones who came to Vermont by choice, and who plan to live here from now on. There aren't any solid figures on how many of us there are, but we're more visible in Chittenden County, where Burlington is, than up in the Northeast Kingdom, where many Vermonters say Vermont is.

The troubling thing about this week is that the schools have been closed. Oh, not by the snow or the cold; those seldom shut down a school. Ice will, but there hasn't been any lately. No, this is what they call winter vacation. It's not a Vermont thing, it happens everywhere. But I think the ski resort people have a secret lobby working on school boards everywhere.

"Let's create a great excuse for family togetherness," they suggest. That means lots of cars with Flatland plates will come here during winter vacation. Rooms and restaurants will fill up, and so will ski lifts, and the Vermont economy will thrive.

I mean, you've got to respond to a chance to create family togetherness, don't you? The question is, precisely how?

Should we go to the slopes and pierce our jackets with metal clips that secure lift tickets, and then parade around as if we'd been decorated for valor? Should we go out and practice the two-stick falldown, and get reacquainted with the feeling of a face-full of snow?

Or should we flee? Florida. Flee. Warm. Sand. Sun. Veg out with a book on a beach.

Here's the problem. Transplanted Vermonters, newcomers, have a tough time running away from winter. You see, we're obsessed with proving that we too are tough enough to make it through a northern New England winter without flinching. We apprentice Vermonters think that if we tough it out, we'll get some kind of grudging approval from the RVs, the Real Vermonters.

Of course we've been here long enough to know that none of them would ever say something like, "Ah, looks like yer gittin usta Vemawnt." That won't happen, but we keep hoping that enough display of tough will bring out at least a kindly thought about us. We hanker after approval from people like Sally Bailey, whose people wandered into the Connecticut River Valley about fourteen generations ago, and have been in Vermont ever since. She thinks that's mostly out of habit. Sally Bailey deals with winter by ignoring it. What panache! How many generations will it take for my begats to do that?

Well, it may be a while, since I can't get my transplanted spouse to embrace those huge two-toned boots that Vermonters wear during the winter. How can you be accepted as a Vermonter in high-heeled patent leather boots that zipper up?

I have evidence that RVs don't share the fixation that your identity as a Vermonter is at risk if you don't hunker down and abide the worst that winter can brew. Certainly Elton Turner doesn't think that way. He and Betty just got back from Florida, and his Vermont credentials are as good as anybody's.

State representative, town selectman, justice of the

peace, dairy farmer, sugarmaker. He's been all those things, and pretty successfully. He's still a sugarmaker. That's about to come into season again, so he and Betty came home.

It would take far more than a little wintry weather to keep Elton from tapping those big maples on a farm that's been in the family for four generations.

They went to Florida right after Christmas for the simplest of reasons. It's cold here. It's warm there. And he doesn't have to milk any more. I suppose when a man has been through more than seventy Januaries and Februaries, and let's not forget March, he no longer has anything to prove about hardiness. In fact I'd be very surprised if it ever occurred to him that there is such a measure of a man, or that others, people from Away, would consider it important.

I'm not that free, even though I know that no Real Vermonter is ever going to smirk at me and say, "Couldn't take it huh?" if I were to go South. But I can't do it. Probation, I guess. Guilt feelings.

My family doesn't think much of that rationale. It would be a nice change, Shiny Boots says. Fort Lauderdale or Clearwater, or even some island. It's not that we want to get out of *here*, they say, but wouldn't it be nice to be *there* for a while, just for a change. Think about bare feet in warm sand instead of frozen toes in two-toned rubberized boots with felt linings.

Yeah, yeah, I say, but this is a special winter. Don't you want to be able to say in years to come "I survived the winter of Ought-Four?"

No, they say.

But we stayed, and we used part of the winter vacation week to explore the things that Vermonters invented or refined long ago, to cope with the season. I tried out a pair of snowshoes, breathlessly. Shiny Boots thought about asking a friend for a ride on a snowmobile, but didn't actually do it. And the skis and skates came out of hiding.

After all, if I'm not at peace with leaving while the daily high temps flirt with zero, then I should be at peace with staying. And living is about more than abiding, just enduring until black-fly season in May. Living means doing, and a Vermont winter offers a lot of scope for that.

Yeah, and I think I'll even go ice fishing. That's it! I'll go ice fishing this afternoon, if no RVs are looking when I try it out. Could be they're onto something good.

Knights of the Snowplow

Cold, like old, is a term defined by perception and self-image.

The Dakotas are full of people who insist that 25 degrees below zero is not really cold. Their self-image is keyed to the notion that hardiness involves shrugging off anything above, say, 40 below. And besides, their bravado is evidence, perhaps proof, that intense cold affects the mind. Frigidity does something to its rational selection of images and ideas. That explains a lot about Dakotans.

In northern Vermont we know something about cold too. The other night one of our quainter villages recorded a -55. Most of the rest of us were at -20 to -30.

At that temperature cars exhale foggy feathers, those that start at all.

Most of them do, but car batteries don't like extreme cold. At -20 some of them allow their starters to say "Rrrr, Rrrr" a couple of times and then sink into hibernation.

Of course if you can crank your car you can drive it out onto a lake where the ice is now two feet thick and would support a locomotive. You can go ice fishing, which involves defying windchill factors and other common-sense cautions. Ice fishing is a cultural thing along the northern edges of this country, and its popularity is additional evidence that deep cold deprives the mind of sound judgment.

It's been snowing a lot too, and that always brings out herds of the most independent, stand-alone small businessmen in all of New England. They are the private snowplow guys. They appear from nowhere after a hefty storm, wearing blades like ancient shields on their pickup trucks and flashing yellow caution lights from their roofs. They contract to clear out driveways and parking lots, and like the ski resort operators, they depend on snowfall. Unlike the ski people, they don't complain in snowless times. Lack of snow means lack of income, but there's too much Vermont in them to say so.

Yesterday I saw a pair of them working the supermarket parking lot. Like jousting knights, they lined up at opposite ends of the lot and charged at each other, snow flying off their blades and spinning up from beneath their wheels/hooves. I thought I'd see bits of flying truck after the impact, but of course they passed each other safely. You see, intense cold affects the mind's selection of images.

It got worse. Suddenly I was seeing them not as armored knights but as those mountain sheep that are always butting heads on the TV nature programs.

On the left, the old herd leader, Henry Lamoreaux, and on the right Reggie Cutler, the upstart. Here they come. Crash!

Images again. It's cold. I wonder if Henry and Reggie ever think like that. After all, Henry drives a Dodge Ram. Bam! Nah, it's too warm in those cabs for minds to drift, and there's too much Vermont in them to permit it.

But Reggie's been talking louder than usual down at the diner, and the last time I noticed that ram on Henry's hood it looked a little groggy. Wonder if they've been truck-jousting. Nah, Vermonters don't do that.

Maybe Dakotans do.

AFTERTHOUGHTS

The Last Illusion

Our loss of innocence may begin with the discovery that the tooth fairy is a fairy story. It continues in small increments, chipping away at the ideas we hold at first firmly, then loosely, then abandon.

Oz is real. No, it's not.

My father knows everything. Oh, he doesn't.

Pete Rose is a hero. No, he's banned.

Big businesses are honest. Name one.

This is a good used car. There is no such thing.

We elect people we can trust. Oops.

Social Security is forever. Oh, yeah?

Little by little our illusions, our notion that things really are the way they ought to be, get stripped away. Verities turn into vagaries, and simple assumptions erode from certainty into doubt and disappointment. There goes another one, leaving what in its place? Realism? Skepticism? Cynicism?

In most cases we emerge from the loss of illusions somewhat less naïve, but not really damaged. Disillusioned need not mean dejected or downhearted.

Instead we discover the soundness of our own judgment, and learn.

I've been a grandfather for a long time. I've been fired and divorced and downsized. I've watched incivility creep into public discourse, ineptitude intrude into public education, and greed feed on sports and business.

I've been shot at (unsuccessfully), tear-gassed (successfully) and have been in cities under air attack on opposite sides of the world with almost a half century between the first and the last. They missed.

I have voted for candidates I thought were good and strong, and have come to regret helping to elect some of them. I've driven cars that have turned into lemons and I've bought home products that fail before the credit card bill arrives.

What illusions do I have left? What fairly harmless beliefs do I hold that are safe from the corrosive embrace of reality?

Not many. I lack confidence that the ozone layer can be restored, that the rainforest can be saved, that extinctions can be forestalled, that loving the Red Sox will ever be painless, or that I will succeed in learning to speak Irish.

But there is a plus side to this dreadful litany. Some things that I believe have not been punctured by the inconvenience of reality.

Some day, for one critical moment, that big bass at that certain secret place in Lake Champlain will stop being smarter than I am.

I believe my sons and daughters will lead useful and productive lives and will seek my counsel when vexed or troubled.

I believe the empty nest is a pretty good place to live, but not alone.

I believe Congress will set aside pettiness and partisan bickering. Well, all beliefs waver.

And I believe in fortune cookies. At least I did until yesterday. I love cracking open those crispy shells to see what silly promise awaits me. Always, the cleverly written little phrases can be interpreted in positive ways.

But not any more. I have lost faith in the fortune cookie. Yesterday I opened one, and found no bland promise of long life and prosperity. Instead I found on that little strip of paper the website address of a computer maker.

My last illusion has morphed into a www.

Jury Service

The call to jury service is a summons, and the only form of public service most people ever do except for voting. Twelve of us are selected and seated, to hear, to ponder, and to render judgment.

The court uses subtle means to impress on us the gravity of our task. We enter through the same door the judge uses, as the bailiff intones, "All rise!" And everyone stands, just as they do for the judge.

The prosecutor says he will prove the defendant operated a motor vehicle while impaired by the ingestion of a chemical, in this case alcohol. The defense attorney says the state has no case.

The only witness is a recruiting-poster state trooper, crisp in uniform and in speech, an utterly believable witness, who says the defendant was driving, was drinking, and was impaired. He leaves no holes.

The defendant admits everything but impairment, and in the absence of chemical test evidence we are left with a case of "he said" vs. "he said."

The judge reads us the law and we retire to deliberate. Seven women and five men will decide whether one man will be free or fettered at day's end.

There are no ground rules for juries, no guidelines. We proceed by reviewing the central theme of our charge; that impairment "to the slightest degree" is sufficient for conviction. We try to resolve contradictions in the testimony. A middle-aged woman wonders how she can get pulled over by the handsome young trooper who testified, and there are chuckles.

But everybody is taking this task seriously. A man's liberty is at stake here. Are we predisposed to believe the trooper just because he's a cop? Is there some factor we're not considering, something we're missing?

This case is at the bottom of the scale of drama and consequence. No courtroom fireworks, no lawyerly brilliance. Just the question all juries must face: Did the State prove its case, beyond a reasonable doubt?

We all agree that it did, after full and sober discussion. I stand in the jury box and answer the judge's ritual question. "Yes, Your Honor, we find the defendant guilty as charged."

We are ushered out before the sentence, and just before we leave the jury room for the last time, a retired school teacher has some words for us.

"I think this is what the old Englishmen had in mind when they invented the jury system," she says. "I have felt ever since the Rodney King and Simpson cases that our justice system is out of whack, but this little case has set my mind at ease. It still works."

She picks up her crossword puzzle magazine and leads us to the elevator, turning in the hall to say she has learned something else. What's that, we ask.

"Defense lawyers wear better suits." Case closed, judgment rendered.

The House on Gimlet Hill

On a slope called Gimlet Hill in Milton, Vermont, there's
an old brick house that's freshly painted.

That's a sure sign that it's just been sold, and that
the new owners are trying to make an "under new man-
agement" statement, a commitment to renovate and
restore.

They have also mowed an unintentional hayfield that
grew up where the grass used to be before the house was
abandoned this last time, and that adds to the impression
that there's some renewal going on.

It's not urban renewal, because Milton is far too rural
for that. Fewer than ten thousand people live here, and
most of those are outside the central village. But it's
renewal just the same.

When the house and the barn behind it were built
New Hampshire's Franklin Pierce was the president of
a country slowly pulling itself apart over the question
of slavery. Japan was being opened to Western trade,
and the Gold Rush was winding down in California. An
ex-congressman named Lincoln was still practicing law
in central Illinois, and the Confederation of Canada was
still two years away.

Milton was then an important mill town on the falls
of an energetic little river, the Lamoille, and it held three
thousand people. (Some of its puffier citizens believe
it's named after the English poet, but most of us think
there's not much distance between "mill town" and
"Milton.")

Well over two hundred mill town men would soon

march away to defend the Union and to shape the legend of Gettysburg. One in ten is still there.

The house built in antebellum Milton was brick veneer over wood framing, and the work was done with skill and care. Hickory pegs hold the big beams in place right where they were put. The timbers and floorboards came from the local forest, and were planed in local mills.

In northern New England, houses are allowed to age with as much dignity as their owners, their temporary custodians, will allow. The house on Gimlet Hill shows the high and low water marks of its endurance.

Rooms have been added as needed, and the house was retrofitted for almost everything considered vital and civilized as the 20th Century progressed: Indoor plumbing, hot water, town water, phone service, electricity, oil heat and finally cable TV.

And in recent years it has aged badly, suffering the architectural equivalent of what the behavioral scientists call failure to thrive. There's too much rot in the windowsills and too much broken glass, too much chipped paint and too many broken bricks.

It doesn't help a house when the owner moves away and rents it to people with no values.

That's why the new coat of paint is important. It's a down payment on a promise to pay attention, to put the house through one more renovation, to enhance its ability to provide the shelter and comforts its designers intended.

The new owners take inordinate pride in a screen door that once again has screening in it, and hangs straight, and closes without scraping the porch floor. It took a lot of work to achieve the simple goal of getting that door to do what it was supposed to do.

The new owners will rip down cheap paneling that

had been painted over, twice, in different improbable colors. They will discover the old wallpaper underneath, all six layers of it. They will spend more money than they intended and they will never finish. It will always be a work in progress. A lot of work, a little progress.

But what could these optimistic and energetic restorers of the Two Thousands learn from their predecessors of the 1890s and even earlier? The house has been through several modifications in the past 150 years.

Who lived here all those years ago? Who planted the giant maple tree out back that once fed four sap buckets in sugaring season?

What child gathered eggs, was scared of the rooster, tended the pigs, milked the cow, rode the horse, tasted the early blackberries just before they were ripe? What lives began and ended, or got shaped within these walls?

Who were the Bradleys and the Pikes and the Neys and the Blairs and all the other former owners who fed their children on what they grew in the garden out back? The town records are silent about most of those families. They have died off or moved Away or married into other families.

Only the house remains, having abided perhaps seven cycles of child-raising, empty-nesting and starting over. When I talk with the elders in my town, I'm always impressed by the way they have processed experiences into wisdom. It would be nice to be able to draw something wise and instructive out of the experiences this old house must have been through in its century and a half.

But you can't interview a house. So the next best thing is to wash its face, clean its body, and cherish it as a symbol of permanence in a landscape where almost everything else is designed to be thrown away.

The Tube and the Human Mind

The other day there was a column in the newspaper, written by a woman who'd been nominated for a literary prize she did not win.

She wrote with sadness of seeing a promotional spot on television in which a teen rips pages out of a book while urging kids to watch MTV.

That follows some widely reported new studies that suggest that very young children should not watch TV at all.

It seems that for the under-two set, those moving images are not only mesmerizing, but somehow get in the way of learning important things like how to pay attention for longer than a few seconds at a time.

The studies say early TV melts the mind, and produces higher levels of attention deficit disorder, and other impediments to thinking and learning.

The clash between the tube and the page for the affection of the human mind is only about half a century old, but it intensifies with an explosion of channels and a series of ratings-driven decisions by programmers.

They're chasing each other toward the junior high school level of humor, defined by pee, poop and puke.

For more than three decades I made a pretty good living as a reporter on TV, and it hurts a bit to be harsh, but the fact is that the social critics are not off-base when they suggest that in this country there's too much channel surfing and not enough page turning, especially among the young.

Congress and the entertainment industry are constantly posturing at each other over who should control what kids watch on TV. The industry has said its Saturday morning programs ought to qualify as educational because the good guys always win; therefore the cartoon dramas should be seen as morality plays.

Baloney.

Last Saturday morning I watched a quartet of muscular heroes in pastel jumpsuits trading lightning bolts with some nightmarish creatures who had vocal cord problems and probably bad breath too. They destroyed a couple of continents in the process of hurling unimaginable energies at each other, and the pastel jumpsuits won because of superior technology and cleverness, not because of superior morality.

There used to be morality plays on the air, programs from which an impressionable young person could indeed draw lessons about the clash between good and evil, about the rule of law, and about justice.

They were TV westerns, the old-fashioned kind, and they used to run in prime time. There were lots of wandering heroes in the early days of TV, and they all had a gimmick. Lash LaRue imposed order with a bullwhip. Hopalong Cassidy had white hair and a limp, and a horse named Topper.

They were *real* make-believe heroes, who fought real make-believe evil, like the rustler, the train robber and the slimy guy who ran the corrupt town. The drifter hero would ride in, try to mind his own business, and within a half hour would have righted a wrong before riding off again, leaving some damsel who'd been rescued waving sadly after him with a white hankie.

The era of the nomadic cowboy hero fizzled out about a generation ago.

Johnny Yuma, was a rebel. He rode through the West.

He also rode off TV after a season or two, in spite

of the macho infusion from Johnny Cash's title song. Johnny Yuma looked like John Denver, and his gimmick was that he wore the scraps of a Confederate uniform. Not enough to keep him on the air.

Paladin, Paladin, where do you roam?

Off into late-night reruns eventually, but only after a good run against type. Imagine a good guy with a used face, who wore black, had a big mustache and handed out business cards. Nah, never work.

But the ultimate wandering hero was the Lone Ranger, especially on radio.

The imagination could always provide the scenes the script hinted at, with the help of sound-effects gunshots and hoof-beats setting the stage in the mind's eye.

A doomsday narration carried the action forward, maybe because the writers weren't very good, especially Tonto's.

"Nnnnh. Me see big trouble in town, Kemo Sabe."

At the end of each episode, Lone would shoot a gun out of some bad guy's hand with a silver bullet, which is probably impossible, and then climb onto the mighty white stallion Silver and ride awaaay!

And the baffled beneficiary of all that heroism would be left standing there holding a souvenir silver bullet, and by the way in those days a silver bullet was neither a can of beer nor a scheme to thwart terrorism, and this guy would ask, "Who was that masked man?"

And the music would sneak in. Dah-dah-dot. Dah-dah-dot, dah-dah-dot-dot-dot. Invariably there'd be some old coot standing around, because somebody had to answer that question, and he'd say, "Shonny, that was the Lone Ranger."

The hero never killed anybody. Bad guys went to jail, where honest sheriffs kept them until honest judges and juries decided their fate, and if they were bad enough they went to the gallows. The system worked, with a little help from broadcasting's first super-hero.

Hi-yo Silver! Awaaay!

A kid could learn about truth, justice and the American way from the TV cowboys. Maybe parents ought to rent some of those old morality plays for their kids on Saturday mornings, instead of abdicating to the merchandisers of "action figures."

The Lone Ranger taught something else too, all those years ago . . . that good music need not be stuffy.

I'm of the generation that cannot hear Rossini's *William Tell Overture* without returning to those thrilling days of yesteryear, even if oh, so briefly.

About the Author

STEVE DELANEY is the middle link in a five-generation family love affair with Lake Champlain and Vermont.

A Vermonter since 1988, and a summer kid since 1947, he classifies himself as a Recovering Flatlander.

Delaney is a fifty-year broadcast journalist who has covered politics and other petty crime in Washington, finance and other felonies in New York and wars on three continents.

He has won national honors for two NBC White Paper television documentaries, and for radio documentaries and news programs produced for Vermont Public Radio, where his distinctive voice has been heard for a decade.

Vermont Seasonings is his first book.